Praise for *Mayhem in Mayberry*

....

"I love this author and I love this book! Brian Lee Knopp is one of the most natural writers I've ever encountered and he tells this all-too-true story with sinewy wit and sublime grace. There are moments in this book where even Knopp seems filled with amazed disbelief at what he has seen, done and lived through. The best narratives should be windows into worlds that most of us will never encounter, and his world most certainly has been one of strange and intimate marvels. I feel lucky to have been let in."

–Elizabeth Gilbert, author of *Eat, Pray, Love*

....

"Brian Lee Knopp is an American original, a fearless standup comedian, and a muckraking master of prose, whose *Mayhem in Mayberry: Misadventures of a P.I. in Southern Appalachia* is one of the funniest and most provocative books I've read in years. It's also a breakthrough chronicle of another America, the hilarious underbelly of crime and betrayal, and the still small possibility of redemption. From the back warrens of the hip New South, to the backwoods of the disappearing American frontier, Knopp manages to unfold the secret tales known only to the best private investigator with stunning prose, and powerful insight. This incredible book conjures the spirit of Raymond Chandler's crime classics to the Carolinas, with the brilliant timing and comic narrative of Steve Martin and David Sedaris. *Mayhem in Mayberry* should be an instant classic—an American classic of an undercover private investigator on the frontlines of crime and laugh-out-loud punishment."

–Jeff Biggers, author of *The United States of Appalachia*

....

"*Mayhem in Mayberry* is the P.I. book you've been waiting for. Waiting, without even knowing you were waiting, because no one would have thought such a book could be written. Yes, read this if what you are looking for is chase scenes, mad dogs and mountaineers all too fond of shotguns. They are here, presented in striking detail, and with compelling rhythm. Cunning and tenacious, Knopp winds his way through Appalachia in search of [...] as helpless presently as [...] shapen by the gods, as any creature Odysseus en[...] nythic heroes, is really chasing his own soul, try[...] d like Odysseus, he keeps finding that elusive [...] in the souls of those he hunts."

**–David Schenck, Ph.D., poet, Questing Beast,
author of *Zchenk Among Demons***

Mayhem in Mayberry

Misadventures of a P.I. in Southern Appalachia

Brian Lee Knopp

Cosmic Pigbite Press

Cosmic Pigbite Press
P.O. Box 2481
Asheville NC 28802
cosmicpigbitepress@gmail.com

Cover design: Kasey Gruen
Cover photo: Brian Lee Knopp
Back cover photo: Ghost Town in the Sky, Maggie Valley, NC.
Courtesy of the author
Author photo: Linda Barrett Knopp

ISBN-13: 978-0-615-30040-5

To Linda—who makes all things possible and worthwhile with just her smile

And to Liz Gilbert—the kindest, funniest Muse ever

Author's Note

All of the events described in this chronicle are based upon actual investigative cases, court documents, and recorded witness statements. All municipal structures, roadways and geographical features referenced herein are real places that I have tried to depict as accurately as possible. The names and biographical details of my clients have been omitted or changed to honor our confidentiality agreements. The names and biographical details of actual individuals under investigation, as well as certain sensitive details of the cases in question, have been omitted or changed to protect their privacy. Any resemblance between the resulting altered identities and actual persons living or dead is coincidental.

CONTENTS

"There are two kinds of people in this world—and you ain't one of them."
–Dolly Parton

PROLOGUE

H er pupils were blown black with stark fear and rage. She was tormented by voices in her head, by the micro-transmitters imbedded in her nose, by my intractable presence before her. She kept raving about, well, everything. How drug cartels had kidnapped and raped her granddaughter. How imposters were trying to gaslight her into an insane asylum by parading about in the bodies of people she knew were dead. How the CIA had killed her childhood friend—an actual former CIA agent whom she hadn't seen in over thirty years—but that didn't matter because they had played Run Sheepie Run when they were little and he had taught her Morse code and she could remember all of it, down to the last detail.

But she had no idea who I was or why I was there.

I was the right person to be there. I was a licensed private investigator, license #1881. I was duly authorized by the North Carolina Private Protective Services Board to perform such duties as locating and interviewing witnesses to crimes or to acts of civil negligence; locating assets; serving civil process; obtaining and preserving physical, video, audio, or computerized evidence on behalf of my clients, be they private individuals, state agencies, law firms, or other corporations. My cost-effective territory was everywhere in North Carolina west of I-77. Yet my licensure afforded me reciprocal rights to work in four neighboring states, as well.

This confrontation shouldn't have been such a big deal. I've chatted up batty people before with good results. With patience, no direct eye contact or sudden movements, and gentle verbal persuasion, I could get them to go where I needed

1

them to go.

That this woman was growling and hissing like a dumpster cat and making short jabbing thrusts with an 8-inch Henckels steak knife—didn't necessarily mean the game was over. Because it wasn't really a fair fight. She was a seventy-one-year-old woman suffering from COPD and incontinence dressed in a faded blue cotton housecoat and big floppy fur slippers. I was a forty-one-year-old physically fit P.I. at the top of my game, a former boxer and martial artist trained in Filipino knife fighting.

But she sure didn't move like an old woman. Her reflexes were quick and erratic like those of a mongoose, and her mind, equally quick and erratic, could still convey much that was true, much that was convincing. Dealing with her was like fighting someone in a phone booth.

The ambulance and paramedics were already waiting outside her immaculate apartment. I just had to convince her that they were on *our* side, they were *our* team, she was not *alone*, they could save her from the agents of her torment if she would just trust me just this once, just please trust me this one time?

The more agitated she became, the more I began sweating this gig as the Very Big Deal it had become. It was turning into the biggest personal and professional challenge of my life. In spite of the hundreds of hours of successful hostile interviews, years of victorious verbal jiu jitsu bouts with lawyers and cops and other pissed off people demented or not—I was extremely close to losing this one. She had one unfair advantage that I couldn't overcome.

She was my mother.

It was a no-win situation. I could succeed as a P.I. and fail as a son, or vice versa, all at the same time. The possibility of getting shanked by my own mother with a Mother's Day gift that I had bought her years before—crouched just beyond my comprehension.

It was all wrong. It wasn't fair. Neither of us deserved to be in such a predicament. I am still trying to figure out why it had to be that way.

This memoir is my attempt to reach an understanding—no, to *accept* an understanding—of why it all had to go down the way it did because of who we were, and are, and always will be.

Chapter One

The Dog I Left Behind Me:
An Asset Repo Story

I followed the double row of ruts in the forest loam for almost a mile. The tracks led me up a forty-five degree incline, through several switchbacks, and finally right up to where the trail dead ended into a head-high earthen mound strewn with boulders, felled trees, unearthed root balls, and empty Mountain Dew bottles. I climbed over this obstacle, picked my way through the slick clay muck and the coils of blackberry thorns and catbriars—and there they were. Maybe.

A 1990 Caterpillar bulldozer looking immaculate but without an engine.

A 1980 Fleetwood singlewide mobile home looking like something that would have made both Edgar Allan Poe and his Raven shit themselves.

Sunk in shade and camouflaged in filth, the structure caught my eye only because the windows seemed to be glaring at me. An ancient black walnut tree loomed over the trailer from behind, its gnarled trunk only inches away from the trailer's rotten skin. The walnut tree had dropped its life-giving load of leaves and nuts on the trailer with such profusion that they now formed furry, lumpy-looking piles on the pitted metal roof, like so many dead beasts awaiting burial.

I was tired and wet and cold and creeped out by the scene before me. I was having trouble thinking of the things I needed desperately to think about in order to get this job done.

It was too chilly even for late September. I felt a low-pressure front slinking down the mountains, bad news to my joints and mood. I felt too insubstantial out here in this damp holler, dressed only in my "realtor" outfit of gray Duck

Head pants, clingy black knit golf shirt underneath a dark green windbreaker stretched over hunched shoulders.

I was distracted by all the debris too familiar yet terrifyingly strange that competed for my fragmenting attention. The rebel flag hanging from the collapsing porch. The carcasses of Chevy muscle cars. Two gleaming customized Harleys, temporary license tags on them both. Tree stumps splintered by bullets, the entire yard littered with spent pistol brass and shotgun cartridges. A brand new Polaris four-wheeler still crouched inside its original packing crate. Hunting arrows bristling from the sides of a cardboard box that sat atop a wrecked vehicle.

And a huge yellow pit bull/Rottweiler mix emerging from the shadows, legging its way toward me. He moved at a stiff, muscle-bound trot. His copper-colored eyes were burning.

The dog was tethered to a frail walnut sapling by a heavy logging chain. As he advanced, the chain uncoiled, and the links started grabbing things: vines, sticks, wires, greasy bits of clothing and skeletal parts of unknown creatures. The sweep of the chain knocked over a water bucket, upended a pair of automotive jack stands, and rolled an orphaned engine block end over end into the red clay mud.

I was in the path of a canine-led Hell-bound train of destruction.

There was no utility hookup. No phone lines. My cell phone's reception had crapped out before I parked at the mouth of the holler. Obviously there was no 9-1-1 address for this place. It wasn't even a *place*, for God's sake! The Unicoi County real property tax scroll denied its very existence. On a topo map, it was just a dark green roadless blob near the Tennessee/North Carolina border, covered with sharply narrowed contour lines leading up to—appropriately enough—*No Business Knob*.

So I wouldn't be found for months if. . . .

Fuck it. Just locate the VIN number on the metal plate near the tongue of the trailer, get the serial number off the 'dozer, and then get the hell out of Dodge.

The air was sullen. The sky sagged in defeat. No creatures called out or moved about. All life was oppressed, plunged into that hushed expectancy of dread that such mountain weather fronts bring. The trailer's black eyes betrayed nothing of what was going on inside. The heavy air pinned my breath to the pit of my stomach. As fog ghosts drifted down the mountain ridge, the only sound was the ghastly rhythmic clanking of metal links paying out behind an increasingly angry dog.

The "What Ifs" attacked me first.

What if that small tree that the dog is tied to is already dead because the chain girded the bark? What if this beast gets aggravated and lunges on the chain one last time and pulls the puny dead walnut tree over and then starts dragging it toward me, barking enough to wake the dead? What if this big mailbox-headed motherfucker knocks over the two Harleys parked outside the trailer with the dangling tree? What if the occupants of this trailer regard me as the bearer of very bad tidings based upon the nature and purpose of my visit? What if one or more of the residents appears on the rotten sagging porch bearing the peculiar features of a crankhead: dead snake breath, rotten teeth, eyes looking like a pair of shiny ball bearings trapped inside two balls of bacon grease? And what if such an individual—who is more than likely a firearms enthusiast—greets me with "Now, just who the fuck you say you was again?" BEFORE he even notices his angry dog and damaged motorcycles?

Clink clink clink clinkclinkclinkclink.

CLANK!

Oh no.

The only "What If" I hadn't pondered, had happened: the dog's tether had snapped midway along the chain.

And he was coming for me at a dead run, dragging ten feet of logging chain behind him.

I was facing Doom, Deadly Dog, and Damnation all at once for $150 and the standard IRS rate for reimbursable mileage.

I was there on behalf of my client attorney's client, a corporation named something like Worldwide Financial Security ClusterFuck L.L.C. This corporation was intent upon repossessing their assets from the very known or unknown individual(s) who had hidden the worthless trailer and who had also made damn sure the 'dozer wasn't going anywhere soon.

Clinkety clinkety clinkety.

To flee through the soggy woods was my first thought. But I just as quickly abandoned it, in light of my pursuer's likely pedigree. It was common for bear hunters in these mountains to take pit bulls and even Rottweilers and breed them with traditional hunting hounds. The goal was to obtain a more powerful, fearless, aggressive dog that will not only run its quarry until it is treed or cornered, but also attack it relentlessly. They would strike out for the bear's back, neck, or hamstrings, biting until they could get a good hold and hang on, keeping the bear hindered until the hunters arrived to kill it. The most sought after quality for these bear dogs besides their game-tracking ability was the quality of being dead game. That is to say, the dog might die from its assault on the bear, but its jaws would remain locked on its foe.

I calculated my odds of winning the dogfight. They were quite poor. I searched for weapons at hand. They were even more disappointing. There were various metal car parts lying around, but they were closer to him than they were to me. I had pepper spray back in my truck. I had no weapons on me more lethal than a three and a half-inch lockblade knife, a Sony dictaphone, and a folding clipboard made of thin aluminum, like the kind cops carry.

I swallowed an acid awareness that, at best, the dog might only take off a hand or a kneecap. Based upon my past experience investigating dog attacks, I had to accept the possibility of losing a few baseball-sized hunks of flesh from my hips, legs, or arms, too. I had one mile to hike out while bleeding heavily and going into shock, and my stupid cell phone would not work when I got to my truck.

The dog was fifty feet away and closing fast. I was more than fifty feet away from the nearest climbable tree and from the trailer itself. My last reflection before pure reaction was how sad all this was, really, because I loved dogs, and I *hated* hospitals *and* finance companies.

When the dog closed to twenty-five feet, I moved.

Clinkety clinkety clinkety.

I ran toward the trailer . . . and straight at the dog. The clipboard was in my left hand, the lockblade in my right. The beast prepared for the joust by hunkering down expectantly, his muscles jutting and coiling under the short tawny coat. His growl made the ground shudder.

The impact of his teeth on the clipboard sounded like a car wreck. With a shiver of his stout neck the crushed clipboard disappeared from my grasp and flew through the air. If I had taken the clipboard and smacked the front of a speeding truck as it passed by, the sight and sound of the clipboard's demise would not have been more impressive. The dog stopped momentarily to inspect his handiwork, pawing at the clipboard's innards: crushed pocket calculator, some broken pens, a shredded yellow legal pad splotchy with dog drool.

I hurtled toward the porch railing and flung myself up and over, crashing onto the flooring like a ton of pit bulls. I looked around wildly for something to use as a barricade against my nemesis. Beer bottles. Jack Daniel's bottle. Pair of socks. Empty carton of Little Debbie Oatmeal Crème Pies. Derelict washing machine. Broken broom. An old iron bed frame, complete with bedrails and box springs. *Yes!* I flipped it over and wedged it length-wise across the porch steps. I picked up my knife and watched the dog digging in and charging towards the porch with renewed effort. I couldn't block off the entire porch. The dog would soon end up here right in front of me. He would either leap four feet into the air to clear the bed frame and bite my face off, or he would jaw and claw the bedframe away from me and start mangling my body.

I would have to kill him to avoid either scenario.

I tried to convince myself that this was just a dog, and not something out of the Book of Revelations.

I got ready. He was getting closer.

"SONNY! QUIT!"

The shout came from everywhere and nowhere all at once, a sound more surreal than the fate posed by the slavering menace hurtling towards me. Down dropped the dog on its haunches, sinking so fast into the weeds that it looked like his feet suddenly deflated like flat tires. He whined and wagged his stumpy tail hopefully, grinning upward.

"Who the fuck are you?" barked the voice again. I turned into its wind.

The voice belonged to a vast bulk standing before me: a shaven-headed, thick-faced, even thicker-bodied man with a sparse blonde moustache and goatee. He was dressed in a black T-shirt with a burnt orange Harley-Davidson logo emblazoned on the front, jeans, and logger's boots. His large head was tilted back and to one side, and his dark blue eyes peered skeptically around the misshapen potato-like snout. His huge arms, sun-reddened and mottled with fading tattoos, were crossed expectantly atop his belly. I found myself replying to these arms.

"I'm Bill Dennison. I'm a realtor"—I shakily handed the man one of my phony business cards that I kept for just such an emergency. He held the card right in front of my face and more than a foot away from his own. He snorted through the busted nose and threw the card onto the porch.

"What are you up to . . . wanderin' 'round here for?"

Then his focus shifted and he looked down the length of the porch.

"God-*damn*. What t'hell you do to my *porch?*"

"Well, I tell you—when your dog went after me, I jumped up here, you know, just trying to save myself. Used that old bed frame to keep him off me. But I didn't do nothing to your dog, Mister. His tether broke and he just went after me as soon as he saw me."

He stared at me meditatively, studying my explanation. Then he lifted a grubby hand in a dismissive wave of acknowledgment: "Yeah, Sonny's chain's busted all to pieces. I put a quick-link in it, but it don't hold." He shook his head in disgust. "Soon as I fix one thing 'round here, something else tears up or goes to missing, one."

His heavy arms folded again, ballooning out from the sleeves of the T-shirt.

"Look here, now, Mister—this place ain't for sale, and none of the land 'round here is, neither. You're trespassing, so you best be off, directly."

"Yessir, I am leaving right now. Sorry to bother you. But now—you sure that dog will let me go? "

"Aw, Sonny won't hurt you none." He thrust his chin toward the dog and called out "Sonny! You a good boy, ain't you, Sonny? Go lie down somewheres."

The dog whined ecstatically at the mention of his name, his stubbed tail wagging so furiously that his whole back end quivered with delight. And then he trotted over to the worn track circling the walnut sapling and lay down.

"'Scuse me, sir—you don't mind if I pick up my clipboard and things that the dog—that I dropped on my way up here?"

His large body turned around slowly, grunting with the effort, and I heard the muttered reply of "Go 'head . . . knock yourself out."

That was just the opportunity I needed.

As soon as he shuffled back inside the trailer and slammed the door behind him, I practically ran to my totaled clipboard, grabbed a surviving pen and a scrap of paper, and scurried toward the tongue of the trailer's frame—where the VIN number was located. I wrote the number down. *Done*. Then a skittish walk towards the 'dozer, swiveling my head from side to side the whole time like an owl, constantly scanning the dog and the windows of the trailer for signs of trouble— and I got the serial number off the 'dozer. *Done.*

When I got back to my truck, the numbers I had inked on the torn and now damp paper were smeared. My eyes must have been pulsing with the beat of my heart because the writing was blurred and jumping around, like trying to read while on a bumpy car ride. But it turned out the numbers were right! I had located my client's assets, but almost at the cost of losing my own.

Chapter Two

The Coolest Job Around

My office was a converted back bedroom in my tiny 70-year-old farmhouse. I could barely squeeze my way in there because of all the packing boxes stacked floor-to-ceiling, each filled with archived case files, videotapes, computer media and other evidence—the sum of my explorations into the plundered and disintegrated lives of strangers. There was enough emotional radiation emanating from those boxes to last several lifetimes. I considered slapping biohazard labels on all of them.

There was a pervasive stench about it all. It might have been that old metal pipe enclosed in an evidence bag—the pipe still plugged with the thigh meat of a man unlucky enough to be sideswiped by a homemade equipment trailer and subsequently impaled by one of the plumbing pipe railings. Or a forgotten pair of underwear from a domestic case that never made it to the DNA testing laboratory.

Or maybe it was just the odor of dubious achievement. I caught a whiff of that every so often, but I ignored it.

I had to.

There are too many areas of investigative specialization to name, and just as many different kinds of P.I.'s to go with them. What unites them all—the successful ones, anyway—is an inner conviction that they *will* find their way through the tumult of lies, confusion, and error, through the maelstrom that passes for modern daily life. They *will* find that proverbial needle in the haystack, the odd grain of sand on the beach, the tiny speck of shit in the Shinola can. And they won't give up until they do.

9

That is to say, to be a successful P.I., your self-confidence has to remain unrealistically high. For sixteen years I had been providing legal support investigations in North Carolina. I had learned to talk my way into and out of any situation you can possibly imagine.

Except one. I never seemed to be able to explain to anyone who was not a P.I. what it was really like to be one.

Something always got in the way. Sometimes I didn't have the time to talk. Sometimes they didn't have the time to listen. Other times, I couldn't talk about the details and they didn't want to hear them even when I could. The reality was always a letdown to all that they imagined the job to be.

I tried to avoid telling people what I did for a living. But the ones I did tell always pulled their eyebrows up in surprise and let their envious smile fall out. Every one of them thought I had the coolest job around.

"No! Are you really? That is sooo cool. I have, like, always dreamed of being a private investigator. I'm really nosey, and I love spying on people, so I think I'd be a good P.I. How do you become a P.I.? Do you carry a gun?"

And so it went. Alas, it seemed that my profession was the apotheosis of a superior culture that was wholly addicted to greed, glamour, extreme behavior, voyeurism, electronic gadgets, and lying—and, as such, would *seem* to have offered an unparalleled opportunity for self-enrichment, no matter where I was located.

But here in the mountains of western North Carolina, surrounded by the corkscrew backroads, tangled forests, and contrary folks native or not—things just worked out differently for me.

Chapter Three

The Bad News Salesman

This is how it started—the strange dance between P.I. and client.

If an individual paid me to find something or somebody, he or she became my private pay client. To satisfy their needs and to keep them confidential, I would do and suffer whatever it took, as long as the whatever was legal, ethical, and did not involve radioactivity.

If that individual hired a lawyer who then hired me, then the lawyer became my primary client, and the lawyer's needs were my main concern. I preferred this arrangement. My investigative objectives were narrowed considerably, and the chain of custody for my evidence was more secure. A private pay had to pass my battery of intuitive alarms that screened for truthfulness, solvency, criminality, lunacy. And after all that, I still had to sweat what a private pay would do with the evidence I gave them—or do to the person(s) implicated by that evidence.

With a law firm as my client, I only had to find out everything the lawyer needed to prevail—or to abandon the matter as a yellow runt dog loser. I could focus on the tasks at hand: locating and interviewing witnesses; conducting video surveillance; identifying stolen or hidden property; performing background investigations; serving civil process documents.

The description above is simplistic, of course. There's no mention of the bewildering diversity of people, plants, and animals with which a P.I. must contend in this rugged region. One minute I would practically be in the 19th century, trying to coax testimony from a wily old Madison County tobacco farmer cultivating his crop with his mule, his dialect a fascinating amalgam derived from the King James Bible, the slang and jargon he learned in the Army, and distilled wisdom from his Scots-Irish forebears nestled in the folds of Belva's hills and hollers before the Civil War. The next minute I would be in the 21st century as I laid out the trail for his neighbor's trailer repossession by plotting waypoints from a GPS receiver and calling them in via cell phone to the repo man from Charlotte, who was simultaneously talking to me and looking at his laptop as he sped down the interstate.

In short, my workaday life was comprised of numerous confrontations with very unreceptive audiences.

Think of it like this. I was a kind of door-to-door salesman. Only I sold products such as "trouble biscuits" or "financial ruin brushes" or some kind of vacuum cleaner—call it the "Whistleblower Vacuum Cleaner"—that actually spewed filth on the user the more they tried to clean with it. Every week I would knock on a door or call on the phone and say, more or less:

> "Hey there, how you doing? Good, I'm doing fine, too. Look, I am trying to involve you in possibly the most sordid, nerve-wracking, humiliating, or costly experience you NEVER wanted to get involved with in your life, to begin with, and CERTAINLY don't have time to get involved with now. But I was just wondering . . . wouldn't you feel better if you spent just a few minutes, hours, days, or weeks of your life by telling me, truthfully and accurately to the best of your ability, your recollection of something that happened weeks, months, or years ago concerning folks you either love and protect, or despise and fear?"

I was a bad news salesman. And over time, such salesmanship efforts took a heavy toll.

Think of me as a kind of priest who needed to hear your confession—in order to save someone *else's* soul.

Think of me as a form of Silly Putty who could be molded to any shape but still retain the imprint of whatever I heard or saw (the distortions would come out when I wrote my final report). I was a hunter of the most predictably unpredictable species of all, and my hours and habits became those of my prey. So intent was I on my pursuit that I did not heed my body's hunger, or its thirst, or its fatigue, or its spine-buckling urge to pee.

I was anything you wanted me to be . . . just so long as you kept talking or kept doing what you were doing. No matter how exhausted I was . . . I listened. I watched. I recorded. I remembered.

Chapter Four

One Question Too Many:
A Field Interview Story

I got a call back in May, 2003 to work a contestable disability claim up near Plumtree in Avery County. The claim had been flagged for further review by the insurance carrier because the loss had been incurred as the result of the prior fire claim (which was covered by a different carrier) and because the insured's injury hadn't been reported within the specified time limit set out in the disability policy.

For this particular assignment, all I had to do was travel about three hours total and conduct a routine, standardized field interview with Tammy Poteet—an interview that supposedly required little imagination and not much more inquisitiveness.

This was just the kind of no-initiative, low-overhead, punch list type of assignment that most P.I.'s craved. The P.I. only had to meet promptly with the claimant or beneficiary, obtain the requested documentation and ask them the necessary questions, write down their answers in the form of a statement, and have the claimant or beneficiary sign the statement.

The client was a competent, no-nonsense insurance claims broker who paid promptly and reasonably well. The company was a reliable source of high-volume, fast-turnaround contestable death and disability investigations. They micromanaged their cases so adroitly that there was little room for investigator innovation and/or error. They supplied all the necessary background information, all the questionnaires and the requested documents checklist.

From the background briefing I had received from my client, it seemed that

Crate and Tammy Poteet had been having a run of bad luck.

First, Crate's landscaping business had been struggling. He could not attract the low-wage Latino laborers that were essential to remaining competitive and earning enough profit to pay off all his brand-new equipment. He had even grumbled to a fellow Christmas tree grower that maybe filing for bankruptcy would give him the competitive edge he needed.

Then, a fire had broken out inside their mobile home, gutting the inside of the trailer just two weeks before Christmas. A kerosene space heater placed in the bathroom to help dry Crate's wet hunting clothes was blamed for the blaze.

And if that was not enough, Tammy had been injured while helping Crate clean up the mess of their melted belongings and the charred twisted metal skin of their trailer. A metal framing bracket had reportedly been knocked loose from the trailer's remains while Crate was using his combination front-end loader and backhoe to scoop up the debris. The 2-lb bracket allegedly fell and struck her on the nape of the neck. She had not gone to the hospital until two days later; she explained that the intense cold outside had kept her from feeling just how badly she had been injured.

Five months after the injury, Tammy had not returned to her full-time secretarial position because of severe headaches, pain, weakness, and intermittent numbness in her dominant right arm. Luckily, the Poteets had fire insurance on the trailer and disability insurance on Tammy.

I mulled over this information as I snaked along the bumpy twisty private road leading up to the Poteet residence. As I swerved this way and that, I recalled thinking about how the experience of driving the mountain backroads always reminded me not so much of locomotion but of *digestion*. You are swallowed into the dark maw of overhanging trees and impenetrable rhododendron and laurel "hells," softened up by the rutted crunching sections of gravel, and squeezed along the convoluted switchbacks drilled and blasted and looped along the nearly vertical walls of rock until you emerge . . . depleted . . . even after traveling one mile. And since so often after navigating some of the more harrowing private roads, the first thing I said to myself when I realized how trapped and vulnerable I would be was "Oh, *shit!*", the digestion metaphor was not . . . forced.

As I drove upward in elevation the woods became thinner, and soon I passed by a small gap in which I glimpsed a man driving a tractor in the clearing. He was long-limbed and dressed in treebark-patterned camouflage hunting cap, blue jeans and red T-shirt. The clearing lay above and a couple hundred feet beyond the thick wall of rhododendrons, hemlocks, ornamental maple and redbud trees that bordered this section of the driveway. I waved at him. He replied with an intense stare and a mouthed cigarette pointed defiantly at me. Then he turned his head away and looked over his shoulder as he backed the tractor towards a 4 x 5 sized round bale of hay. With a revving of the engine and a belch of exhaust, the tractor lurched backwards and thrust the hay spike attached to the tractor deep into the bale's core. He worked the tractor's hydraulics, lifted the spike and the skewered hay bale a foot or two off the ground, and then drove away with the hay.

As the driveway tunneled through the wooded entrance of the property and curved towards a cleared, gently rolling pasture, the sound of my truck crunching its way up the gravel drive alerted some dogs. I heard them cut loose with deep bellows of alarm way before I could see them. Once I completed the last blind turn of the driveway, I finally saw the kennel sitting a few yards back into the woods. It was a nice kennel. It had chain-link fencing, a concrete slab floor, and six spacious partitions each with their individual wood-framed dog house. The top of the entire kennel was covered with a heavy-duty blue plastic tarp which helped keep the snow and rain from soaking the slab and the harsh sunlight from baking the dogs in early spring, when the leaves had not yet sprouted to create their own shade. But it was now late May, a few days before Memorial Day, and the dogs seemed to glow amid the comfortable shade cast by the heavy foliage.

The dogs were fine-looking Treeing Walkers, white, black and tan-colored hunting dogs that resembled beagles—that is, if only beagles were a foot taller and almost two feet longer, thirty pounds heavier, and worked out daily with weights. The Walkers' deep baying was deafening – ba-ROO! Ba-ROO! Ba-ROO! As I drove past them, the dogs paced inside the kennel on legs stiff with challenge and authority, their tails arched rigidly over their backs, their noses working over my arrival.

I was pleasantly surprised to see such a considerate and rather costly environment for these dogs. Their fellow mountain-bred hunting dogs normally spent most of their lives neck-chained to a tree, with an open-ended plastic 50-gallon barrel half-buried on its side in the dirt for a shelter. When the dogs were not lunging away from their tree tethers and barking at anything that they scented or heard, they were otherwise barking and lunging *towards* some tree because they'd chased a 'coon or bear up there. There was a poignant symmetry to their tree-based life.

I was even more surprised to see the even nicer new A-frame house with the bright green standing seam metal roof and wrap-around deck. Bundles of framing lumber and cedar siding were stacked near the stairway to the front deck. There was a debris pile of spent tubes of caulk, cardboard boxes, and scrap lumber heaped upon the blackened section of ground that marked the site of the fated mobile home.

And I was more surprised still to notice a very grim-looking Tammy Poteet staring at me with doe eyes as I walked up the stairs leading to the deck.

I smiled when our eyes met. She flitted away from the double sliding glass doors in response. Before I cleared the last step to the deck, she opened the front door to let out an obese rust-colored Chow, who greeted me enthusiastically, puffing with the effort, his black tongue rapidly dipping in and out of his mouth, his curved thickly-fringed tail fanning the air around us. I lowered my hand, palm out, to let him figure things out, but he ignored my hand and circled my knees instead, snuffling avidly, a furry vacuum cleaner.

"Sid's okay . . . he's just a big ole nosy dog. Aren't you, Sidney?"

Sidney stopped inhaling my pants for a moment as he turned towards the woman and grinned, wagging his entire rear end in agreement. Then he resumed his forensic breathing.

"Oh, that's all right. I have dogs, can't hide that fact from another dog. Are you Miz Poteet?"

"Yes . . . Tammy."

"Okay, Tammy. I'm Brian Lee Knopp, the investigator who talked to you yesterday on the phone."

"Yes, Mr. Kanupp, I was expecting you. C'mon inside."

"Do those Walkers down there know how good Sid has it up here?"

She gave me a tight smile and an enigmatic reply: "The Walkers are my husband's . . . Sidney's mine."

I walked inside and saw a beautifully finished cabin interior. High ceiling, real plank paneling, carpeting in the living room and on the stairs leading to the loft; ceramic tile in the kitchen where a large throw rug bearing a "U.K.C. – Hunting Dogs" logo on it lay prominently; immaculate hardwood flooring in the dining room. A fieldstone fireplace embraced by a huge hemlock beam mantelpiece dominated the north corner of the living room. Dog trophies crowded the mantelpiece.

Tammy moved slowly and deliberately. She turned her whole body in the direction of her focus, rather than swiveling her head. Her shoulders were visibly hunched, her head tilted slightly upward. She exhibited the protective posture P.I.'s refer to as "turtle head." She might have been acting, but there was something about the look in her eyes that made her discomfort quite convincing. Yet on the other hand, her face was not "moon faced" from steroids, nor did she have that glassy, lethargic look of someone on heavy pain meds. She asked me where I would like to sit and I gestured towards the oak dining room table.

Straight off I saw the shotgun. I am always keen on locating weapons when I am in someone else's home, and in the mountains I am rarely disappointed. The shotgun was an expensive-looking long-barreled 12-gauge pump-action type. It was a wild turkey gun, with full sight rail and a treebark-style camouflage finish covering the entire weapon. The shotgun was leaning next to an antique dining room hutch filled with mixing bowls, tureens, and little porcelain figurines. I spied the glint of a shotgun shell's brass peeping out from the gun's magazine tube. I had no idea if there was a shell in the chamber, ready to go. For reasons known and yet unknown, I positioned myself at the far end of the table, close to the sliding glass doors, a position with better access to the shotgun than anyone else except maybe Sid the Fat Chow, who had returned mysteriously from outdoors in order to slump to the floor underneath the table with a heavy grunt and sigh a fall asleep.

I set down my aluminum folding clipboard and took out my paperwork. I repeated the explanations for the interview that I had given to her over the phone yesterday, stressing how routine and simple the interview would be. She blinked her eyes rapidly and dipped her head ever so slightly—not quite a full nod—to confirm her acquiescence in the role as the interviewee. While I was talking and fussing with papers that kept slipping off the mirror finish of the oak table and gliding onto the glossy red oak flooring, I slid a few consent forms at her and casually mentioned that she could sign these before we got started. She signed them and then asked me if I would like some sweet tea, and I said sure even though I hate the stuff, and she made two of them, tall glasses filled to the brim with tea-colored columns of cracking ice cubes.

I notice that she carried only one glass at a time. I made a mental note to write that down later.

Claimant did not carry glass of tea with her weakened/injured right arm; made extra trip to avoid doing so.

And before we even got started with the interview proper, Tammy Poteet was quietly freaking out.

She had warm tired brown eyes. Her eyes seemed too large for the small face and for the cupid-bow mouth that kept trying out several faltering smiles a minute but gave up each time because the eyes wouldn't go along with the charade. Her brow was furrowed and her lips pursed as if in determined thought. Her thin frosted blonde shoulder-length hair accentuated the heavy layer of bronzer on her face. Pain had walked on her thirty-six-year-old face with heavy crow's feet and etched deep lines through the tanning makeup. Her face was a fallen brown leaf.

She rose slowly to her feet to retrieve a cushion and told me to use it for the hard-seated chairs –"It seems like when you buy them they're not broke in yet." The gesture was spontaneous, yet she performed it so mechanically, without really considering whether I wanted the flat pillow or not, that it struck me as a rehearsed gesture to cover up her very palpable nervousness. I thanked her for the pillow anyway, and waved my arm in a sweeping motion at the house and complimented her and her husband for being able to rebuild so quickly and elegantly. This compliment splashed on her like a cold ocean wave. Her entire body stiffened and she rocked back slightly on her feet before sinking slowly back down on her chair. She let out another fugitive smile that was quickly caught and imprisoned again by the still unexplained gravity of this situation. She declared: "Oh, the house is a mess. I can't keep up with it."

I looked again around at the spotless interior and thought *Southern Living* might be coming by later for a photo shoot.

But I understand what you mean. . . you've been hurt and all,
'use."

..n is still judged by the way she keeps her home!"

..d this so forcefully, without any pleading in her voice and yet with so
..i pleading in her eyes, that I didn't know how to respond. I just nodded and
stared at my paperwork.

Once she had signed the consent forms, I gathered them up and shut them
inside the folding clipboard. At the same time, I activated the digital recorder
hidden inside the clipboard. The digital recorder was connected to an omni-
directional microphone, the head of which peeped imperceptibly through a small
rivet hole located on the surface of the clipboard's aluminum shell. Tape recording this interview was unnecessary, because at the end of this interview, I had to
show my interview summary statement to the interviewee, anyway. They either
signed off on its accuracy right then and there or they didn't and you rewrote the
statement accordingly. When I first saw the man on the tractor, followed by the
sight of the loaded turkey gun, I decided to write my *own* insurance policy for this
interview, a policy that would cover this cookie-cutter assignment for exactly one
hour, seven minutes and thirty-nine seconds of digital recording time.

I began to talk with her about her accident, her medical history, her current
complaints. I told her how sorry I was about the fire, and she creased her mouth
and fluttered her eyelashes in gratitude. All the while she was talking, she was
sliding her wedding ring off and on her finger, rotating it endlessly, or tapping the
glass of opaque icebound tea. Her eyes were wet cups of worry.

The interview proceeded slowly, haltingly. After a half hour or so, she had
calmed down a bit; she had stopped fidgeting with her wedding ring and had even
managed a full smile. She tried in earnest to remember past medical care provid-
ers, illnesses, prescriptions. She denied smoking, yet there was a faint smell of
cigarettes in the room, and there were glass ashtrays all over the house.

She left the table for a minute to go rummage around in a cabinet next to the
refrigerator, and she offered up some documents to help speed up the interview—
a gesture for which I was unspeakably grateful. I remember thinking: *five or ten
minutes more and I'll be finished with this gig . . .*

The front door opened. The man on the tractor was now striding through
the entrance, and the door somehow slammed shut behind him without being
touched. I don't know whether it was the air-tightness of the house or the scary
vibe coming off the man or both—but the whole house just sucked inward, out
of breath, sucker-punched by the arrival of Crate Poteet. His eyes bulged with
accusations that I imagined were sadly wasted on this particular instance: his wife
and I were fully clothed and had an oak table between us. Hearing the front door
slam and seeing the presence of the man, the fat dog lumbered up onto his paws,
and with toenails clicking frantically to gain purchase on the hard shiny floor, Sid
beat a hasty retreat from underneath the table and headed for the far end of the

kitchen, near the glass double doors. He curled up right next to the shotgun.

Crate walked quickly through the house and towards me. "You Mr. Canipe—the private investigator?" He asked in a deep, brassy voice filled with disbelief, his already pop-eyed countenance looking more aggrieved, as if I should have been somebody else or *somewhere* else.

I stood up and introduced myself, staying behind the table as I did so. He stepped forward, and when I was within the reach of those long reddened arms he shook my proffered hand dispiritedly, a weak handshake which was not that uncommon among men in the mountains and by itself meant little. He wasn't wearing his baseball cap now, and his hair was a coppery buzzcut that gave him the look of a lean razorback hog. He did not have little piggy eyes, though, no, not at all. His were bright blue splashes spilled on onion bulbs. The veins near his temples twitched and pulsed, and the striated muscles in his jaw fluttered and clenched like he was chewing something. His sunburned head was narrow but the thin veal-colored mouth was gashed wide across his face and shaped in the manner often referred to as cruel by those who found out the hard way: wives and children and pets on the receiving end of its down-turned malevolence. He dipped his hand into his shirt pocket, plucked a cigarette out of the pack of Marlboro Lights and fired it up. His next question was snorted at me on the exhale.

"How come all this is taking so long? You said on the phone this wouldn't take but a few minutes?"

I told him that we were almost finished, and as I looked towards Tammy I nodded to reiterate our sense of accomplishment. There was no response from Tammy. She was now a carved statue, a stage prop, a distant sad memory. All that was left alive were her liquid eyes, but they were evaporating, also, the last of her essence vanishing slowly like the grin on the Cheshire Cat.

The routine nature of this case was fading, also.

Crate nodded tightly to himself, and proceeded into the kitchen and poured himself a Mountain Dew that was also crammed with ice cubes. He walked back towards the dining room table and stood next to Tammy's hologram of herself. As he stood there, he alternated between puffing on the cigarette and crunching ice cubes. And from where I was sitting, I could see that he was taller than I feared, at least 6' 3", train-rail thin and just as hard-looking. His arms were two rust-speckled crowbars attached to his shoulders.

I somehow returned to my sitting position—the flat pillow had fallen to the floor unnoticed by the Poteets—and resumed my questions. She answered in a faltering voice, occasionally looking toward her husband for confirmation. He did not return her look. Instead, he threw one of his blood-colored meat hooks across the table and snatched the ashtray towards him and pounded the stubs of his cigarette into it repeatedly. The abruptness and violence of the gesture made Tammy's entire body shudder.

He then tossed his drinking glass up to his mouth and sucked in some more ice to crush with his bunched jaws. While crunching away, he studied the palms of his hands like he had just noticed them for the first time. He set down the glass and bent towards the table and removed a lockblade knife from his rear pants pocket. He flicked the knife open and leaned back in his chair and began cutting the calluses from his palms, the parings of flesh falling to the previously spotless floor. I forgot my line of questioning for a moment, distracted by the worrisome possibilities presented by a hot-tempered man with a lockblade sitting less than a rangy arm's length away from me and his fearful wife.

When I resumed my questioning, Tammy was practically whispering her replies. I always saved the easiest questions for the beginning and the end of an interview, to help them to get started and then to give them a sense of relief when they finished. Today, I finished up with questions so throwaway that even Crate snorted appreciatively while he pretended to ignore us.

"Are you now or have you ever been engaged in any high-risk activities such as flying a plane? Skydiving? Hang-gliding? Race car driving? Unlimited hydroplane racing? Mountain climbing? Mountain biking? Boxing, wrestling, full-contact karate, kickboxing, or any professional martial art?"

After she answered the final question, I finished writing it down. Then I gave her the four-page statement that I had prepared based on her answers. I told her to please read it for accuracy, and then sign it—and we'd be done.

"Lemme see what you've told him, here."

Crate snatched up the pages and read, and his burning mouth flickered over the words. Several minutes dragged by, and he had only made it to the second page when his face began to flush an even darker wine-red, and his nostrils flared. He started shaking his head and he dropped the pages and fired both blue-eyed barrels at me as a warning shot.

"You mean to tell me . . . you come all the way out here . . . to ask us the same stupid bullshit questions we've done answered *three* times already? A whole *six months* have gone by, and the in-surance people are still dragging their feet . . . and now they're wanting to know what for my wife went to the doctor's office— *ten years ago*? I don't know . . . but it seems to me you are either stupid as hell or calling us liars, one. Now which is it?"

"Well, Mr. Poteet, as I said before, it is a routine follow-up to have a field interview. I am sorry to inconvenience you two—I'm just following their procedures, it's not my doing. Between you and me, insurance companies can be aggravating at times. They have a funny way of doing things before they settle up with you, that's for sure."

"So you're not with the in-surance company?"

"Nosir. They hire me as an independent contractor—just like you would with your landscaping business."

His eyes narrowed and his jaw jutted with suspicion.

"How'd you know I was in the landscapin' business?"

"They told me that when they gave me the assignment."

"Well if they told you that much for no good goddamn reason, why the hell didn't they tell you they've asked us all these questions?"

"Mr. Poteet—I have *no* idea. Here's what they told me: you had a fire loss before Christmas; that your wife was hurt and out of work for almost half a year, and that you were the sole provider, a self-employed landscaper. They tell me what they want to tell me, and I've got no control over it. I get the assignment and the instructions through the FAX machine and it's off I go. Just the way it is when you deal with a big company, I guess. But I try to get it done as quick as possible and bother people as little as possible."

He rubbed his chin with the back of his hand, reflecting on my excuse.

"Hell, then, it's no wonder why in-surance cost so much . . . how those people can even breathe with their heads so far up their own asses, I don't know . . . ."

A good sign. He's trying to be funny. Try to get them back on your side now, so she will sign the forms and you can leave.

I risked a smile and an appreciative chuckle. "You know, Mr. Poteet—that's a real good question—one I wished I'd thought of myself before I took on these kinds of assignments." I grinned a bit wider and cast a quick glance at Tammy. Judging by her demeanor, she had become one with the oak chair.

The room took a quick breath, and I used the chance to calm them both down with a digression. I let my gaze float over toward the fireplace and settle lightly on the dog trophies. I mentioned that, as a by-the-way comment, on my way up here I had been admiring the Treeing Walkers, and judging from those trophies, I'm not the only one who felt that way about them.

The change in Crate was almost audible. His body relaxed; his jaw and neck slackened, and the circumferences of his eyes softened. The eyes themselves were no longer like round metal dies used for stamping out parts, but rather like soft organs devoted to seeing things. His shoulders rounded down and his whole countenance lost its menace. He even grinned as he started talking about blood lines and dog trials. When he flagged a bit, I prodded him some more.

"Yessir, if a man couldn't tell how good those dogs are . . .one look at all those trophies would show him, wouldn't it?"

He grinned toothily, and lit up a post-canine conversation cigarette. He was nodding pleasurably to himself, blowing smoke towards his wife, who responded to her husband's convivial carcinogenic gesture by actually returning to this physical dimension. She pursed her lips and her eyes widened with her awareness of a new reality in the room.

It's working I hoped. *Just one more conversational gambit, then I get the statement signed and flee.*

"You must compete a lot to win so many trophies! Are those all from just this year?"

"Oh, hell no. Those trophies go back, oh, 3-4 years at least."

The understanding sparked like a live wire torn loose inside me.

"The trophies go back, oh, 3-4 years at least. . ."

They had a total fire loss five months ago . . .

You know damn well those trophies would have been proudly displayed in their trailer that burned downed . . . accidentally. Trophies that are made of plastic. Trophies that will melt into goo long before all the paper burns, before the paneling peels apart, before the carpeting cooks off and the structure chars and collapses onto itself.

Trophies that could not have a survived an "accidental" fire . . .trophies that were removed for safekeeping before the "accident" happened.

This cookie-cutter case was crumbling to pieces.

Then I started to quietly freak out.

Oh, no! Now what? Do I pursue this? Do I flesh it out with questions about where the trophies were kept? This could be arson fraud! And I have the tape recorder rolling—and about fifteen minutes or more of recording time left.

How big of an investigator do I want to be right now, in this dicey situation? Do I just deal with the here and now disability claim? That's all I'm getting paid for. But doesn't one good fraud lead to another? How did Tammy Poteet really get hurt?

I didn't have the time to answer these questions for myself. Even under the strictest self-discipline, and in spite of the direst of consequences, I cannot keep a poker face. I was born with and am continually cursed by a pinball machine face. So try as I might to suppress my awareness of Crate's intriguing admission, Crate saw "TILT! GAME OVER" flashing at him from my eyes.

And Crate realized his mistake. So now his face hardened again into burgundy saddle leather, and he commenced to ride roughshod over me.

"I don't understand why we have to go through all this bullshit again. It's a form of harassment, that's what this is! We've paid up our premiums; we've given them the forms twice now; we've given statements about the fire to the po-lice, to the fire department, to the county fire marshal, to the in-surance adjuster—to every goddamn person that you could think of."

He pointed a burning cigarette and an equally smoldering finger at me.

"Now here you come, playing dumb, asking us all about everything all over again, trying to trip us up so the in-surance company can beat us out of our dollar. And now we're having to jump through all the same hoops for Tammy's dis-bility! It's un-real! That's what this is . . . *un*-real!"

"Well . . . I tell you what, Mr. Poteet—I won't take any more of your time today. I appreciate your situation, and regret that you've been given a runaround, and I don't want to be guilty of that, myself. If Tammy will just sign these forms, I'll take them with me and be out of your hair right now."

"Nooo, uh-uh. That statement is staying right *here* . . . there's too much personal information in there, and until we get someone from the in-surance company here in person, we're not turning over nothin' to nobody *no more!*"

"I understand. But Mr. Poteet . . . that statement doesn't say anything more than what you've already told the insurance company—isn't that what you've been telling me all along? That you've been answering the same questions? So all we need to do now is have it signed to show that *I* have met with Tammy and interviewed her personally about all of this, and it's a done deal. Basically, I need that form to get paid . . . to show that I have done my job!"

Crate blinked a few times, confused for a second or two by the angle I was trying to work. He snuffed out his cigarette, and when his thoughts returned to him, he replied:

"I understand you're trying to do your job and all, and I'm not trying to keep you from getting *your* money—even though that's what the in-surance people are doing to us."

"Tell you what . . . give me the name of your boss, the in-surance man who sent you here, and give me his phone number. We'll call him and tell him you came here, so you can get your money. . . and we'll tell him we're not sending no forms until *we* get *our* damn money."

Think, Brian. Should you let him call the client? What will that do? Do you want to be trapped here even longer, listening to a possible ugly phone call, and you being the only warm target for his frustrations besides Tammy? Should you just walk away from it and admit defeat? Would that be wimping out? Would wimping out be such a bad thing right now, anyway? The man lost his house, just finished building a trophy home, his business is doing poorly, and now his wife can't contribute, he's backed into a corner . . . safer to let him out. He does have nice hunting dogs . . . . seems to care for them . . . . but how does a struggling landscaper build a trophy home? What about those dog trophies? Why is his wife so harum-scarum?

And then—talk about the Imp of the Perverse! I got pissed off.

I was angry about the whole conflicting Poteet-world thing—the possible fraud angle, the possible domestic violence angle, everything. The attempt to bully me and shame me in front of my "boss" so I could get my pay, bullying Sid the Fat Chow. To hell with him and his bloody lobster's claws and his lockblade and his turkey gun!

I was trapped, too—by this house, by this remote location, by the looping intestine of a private road, by my own inclination towards stubbornness at the worst possible times. And that was a dangerous thing all the way around. The client's instructions were "don't be confrontational." But what else was I there for, then, but to confront? My very presence there, my need for a signed statement—it was all confrontational!

Without giving in, I gave it one last shot. I wanted to get him to read the statement and voice his objections to it, because that would be recorded evidence of his refusal to allow me to complete the field interview. I already got Tammy to sign the consent forms, forms which waived her right to protest the release of the very information she—or rather her husband—refused to relinquish.

"Mr. Poteet—I'm sorry, but that's not the way I do things. I'll make an exception—just this once—for you in that: if you or your wife will go back through that statement and tell me exactly what you find objectionable, and also tell me exactly how the insurance company has not handled your claim in a reasonable, professional manner—I will make sure that the insurance company knows about that so they can get their act together and so you won't have to keep being bothered by any more questions. Will that be okay?"

That was a white lie. I feared that it was a provocative one, at that.

The resulting explosion was predictable, but impressive all the same. Yet like many angry men, his voice was filled so full of rage that its menace lay in its subdued, faltering, breathless delivery, its danger diverted into every vocal crack and choke and spume.

Crate Poteet was a volcano about to blow.

"You. Know. What? I smell . . . *shit*—you know that? That's what I smell. Some shit. And you know what else? When I smell shit, I've either *stepped* on it, or I'm looking *right* at it. I know what you're getting at, goddammit to hell . . . . I *sure* do . . . I *sure* do . . . fucking in-surance companies . . . take your money before the day is done. . . and what do you get in return? NOT A FUCKING THING! Bunch of goddamn hoops to jump through, that's all there is to it . . . bills you can't pay, can't get back to living your life until those sonsabitches SAY you can . . . what the *hell* was I makin' . . . those goddamn payments for . . . to deserve *this*. YOU TELL ME! Goddamn companies . . . makin' money hand over fist . . . that's right . . . and if they get a 10% loss from people they say are stealing from them, why they just go . . . and pass it off on us, take it out of the hide of the 90% that's done nothing wrong . . . the people who only wants to pay their bills and everything! If I was some goddamn illegal Mex'kin who don't speak English, I would have been paid up in full a month after it happened . . . and you wouldn't have said 'Boo' to my wife about the whole thing, neither! "

And then the red-headed volcano *really* blew it.

"I'm not readin' ONE. FUCKING. THING. And neither is Tammy! And she ain't *signing* nothing, neither! This whole pile of shit with the in-surance has taken enough of our time and caused us enough aggravation to last two lifetimes! And I need to get back to work this afternoon . . . make me some money so's we don't starve to death. . . *and I need Tammy to help me lay down some mulch before it rains.* So this whole business is over and done with."

Before the full impact of his admission could hit him—that his wife was capable of performing physical work while pursuing a disability claim—Tammy broke in with a weirdly melodramatic cry that escaped from her otherwise expressionless face:

"O DEAR LORD! CRATE! THEY THINK WE'RE *STEALING*!"

I looked at her in amazement, and with not a little horror. It was as if a bathroom wall picture had come to life and yelled "YOU DIDN'T WASH YOUR HANDS!"

The implication of wrongdoing was like a bad smell in the room that we never actually discussed. Now, though, with the imputation of fraud hanging palpably in the air, the stench became unbearable, as if a rotting carcass had been slipped under the dinner table.

With Tammy's utterance of "stealing," Crate cut his eyes towards me, then dropped his focus past my shoulder—towards the turkey gun.

The prospects of having a gun drawn against you is difficult to deal with, more so because of the unreality rather than the yet unfulfilled finality. As Americans, we all know our well-rehearsed lines, the Hollywood bravado and defiance, the flippant challenge and the bad guy's backdown. But somehow in real life it is much different. Because when you stare at the ridiculously small metal cylinders or piece of black pipe that will unleash a demon who will eat your life bite by bite with loud gulps of fire and leaden teeth—it is too preposterous to believe.

Oh, c'mon, surely not me, not now—I don't have time for this . . . .

But a gun that's just within reach of an angry man *in his own home*—that's the stuff from which nightmares and widows are made.

And there's something about the face of an angry man whose rage has reached such a state of resolution that their face becomes a death mask: bone-tight, eyes rigid with irrevocable purpose. To look at that face, you are no longer sure if you are still staring at a human nemesis or at The Grim Reaper himself.

Crate Poteet was just such an angry man.

Moving fluidly yet unhurriedly, I gathered up my belongings and got up from the table without saying a word, pushing the chair back as far as I could with my butt so the chair trapped the shotgun. I stepped over the Sid the Fat Chow Dog, opened the sliding glass door and said "Thank you for your time, Mister and Missus Poteet." I seemed to be floating over the deck and down the long flight of steps. I did not hear my footfalls, because my ears were filled with the expectation of the dreaded chak-CHUNK of a pump shotgun being readied to fire.

What I first heard was the click of my key turning in the ignition . . . and then nothing. I tried it several more times. Nothing. I tried my best car-coaxing incantation: *C'mon baby . . . c'mon darlin', we're both gonna be target practice for somebody unless you get going . . . .* I threatened my truck with firebombing, with submersion in the Nolichucky River, with no oil changes *ever* again. Nothing.

There was activity at the Poteet house . . . the front door opened . . . Sid the Fat Chow Dog waddled out . . . and barked at me.

I turned the key and the truck started.

I drove away with one eye looking ahead, the other scanning the rearview mirror for signs of pursuit. There were none.

I think Sid might have saved me that day.

Chapter Five

The P.I. as Sand Sucker:
Interviewing Witnesses

Interviewing witnesses was usually my most rewarding investigative effort—and usually the most challenging. I got a rush every time I had to match wits with mountaineers, the most cunning, versatile and entertaining oral culture left in the country.

My friend David, a former investigator for the Buncombe County Public Defender's office and Asheville native, had likened the process of extracting truthful testimony to "sucking sand up a soda straw." It was hard work, took forever, you didn't get much, and what you got tasted awful and couldn't be swallowed, anyway.

In North Carolina, P.I.'s don't have state-granted powers of coercion and control (read: sanctioned threats and intimidation). If your party shuts the door or hangs up the phone—game over. You lose. Or at least that's how it was in the game I played. Some P.I.'s played much differently.

At the end of the day, if a P.I. can't count on a warm body taking the stand or otherwise giving sworn, convincing testimony that is favorable to his or her case, they can forget about all the James Bond gimmicks and gadgetry. A credible witness is the most valuable kind of evidence to find—and evidence so rare and so easily lost that even the most arrogant trial lawyer will eat holes through his own stomach worrying about his witness.

A witness like Mr. Hunnicutt, for example.

[Transcript of Telephone Interview with Witness Dwayne Hunnicutt]
6 January 2003

HUNNICUTT: "Hello?"

BLK: "Yessir, could I speak to Mr. Hunnicutt?"

HUNNICUTT: "You got one of them. Which one you want?"

BLK: "Uh, Dwayne Hunnicutt?"

HUNNICUTT: "Big one or little one?"

BLK: "Well, I'm not exactly sure of the size I'm looking for [laughs]. . . I guess I would like to speak to Mr. Hunnicutt senior."

HUNNICUTT: "That'd be me. I'm the old one—and the big one, too. My son Jeremy Dwayne is the littler [sic] one, but he goes by Dwayne, too."

BLK: "Okay. Mr. Hunnicutt, I'm calling regarding the fatal dog fight that occurred last month on Big Pine Creek Road, involving—"

HUNNICUTT: "Uh huh, you don't have to say no more. I know all about it [chuckling]."

BLK: "Oh, that's great. Well, do you mind if I ask you a few quest–"

HUNNICUTT: "Who did you say you was again?"

BLK: "Brian Lee Knopp. I am a private investigator here out of Asheville, and–"

HUNNICUTT: "—Brine [sic] Canipe? A private investigator? From Asheville?"

BLK: "Yessir."

HUNNICUTT: "You're kind of like that feller who works with Madlock [sic] on the TV show? You're [inaudible, coughing], right?"

BLK: "Uh, well, I guess so, I don't know. I've never seen that show."

HUNNICUTT: "You haven't? It's a good show, now. You ought to watch it—you could learn a thing or two [inaudible, laughs]. Who [coughing, inaudible]--"

BLK: "I'm sorry—could you repeat that?"

HUNNICUTT: "I asked you who you are a-workin' for?"

BLK: "Well, Mr. Hunnicutt, in the interest of remaining fair and confidential, I'm not really supposed to tell who my client is—"

HUNNICUTT: "[Chuckles]. Why, I'd expect you to say something like that. I know good and well you're helping one side against the other. A private investigator ain't nothin' but a lawyer's gopher. He's any man's dog who will hunt him, if the price is right. Am I right or am I right?"

BLK: "Well, Mr. Hunnicutt, I'm not sure [inaudible] . . . I do work for an attorney representing one of the parties, and—"

HUNNICUTT: "—lemme tell you something about it: I'm not going to jump in no hole until I see one side of it or the other. Just tell me whose side you're on and see how we get along then."

BLK: "Uh, I'm not on anyone's side, Mr. Hunnicutt. I need to hear the truth of what happened, no matter how it plays out. If you want to tell me the truth of what you know, then it doesn't really matter which side I'm on, now does it?"

HUNNICUTT: "Oh, I'll tell you the truth, all right. But you don't want to talk to me about this mess."

BLK: "Oh? Why is that?"

HUNNICUTT: "Nosir, you don't want to hear me tell of it. I won't give you all that smiley-faced [sic] lawyerin' [sic] talk. I'll stand up—right there in the courtroom—and tell it like it is and shame the devil. That's just how God made me. I won't bow down nor cleave my tongue in two for nobody. You understand what I'm a-telling you?"

BLK: "Yessir. I appreciate your honesty, and your willingness to tell the truth—that is why I would like to talk to you about this dog fight, because other folks are afraid to get involved."

HUNNICUTT: "Well, first off, [coughing] got it wrong: it warnt [sic] no dog fight."

BLK: "It wasn't?"

HUNNICUTT: "No! Hell no! Warnt [sic] no fight! That little bitty dog no bigger than my nose, going up against that Rock-wiler [sic] big as a bear? Not much of a fight a-tall, in my book. Nosir, I wouldn't call it a fight, anyway."

BLK: "Okay. Tell me what you saw, then."

HUNNICUTT: "Lemme [sic] ask you one question, first. Am I going to have to appear in court about this?"

BLK: "Well, Mr. Hunnicutt, I won't lie to you . . . anytime you witness an accident in which someone gets hurt or loses their pets or livestock or suffers property damage . . . there's a chance that you might have to show up in court and tell what you saw, yessir."

HUNNICUTT: "I'm not going to court. And young feller [sic], you can just close your book on that chapter."

BLK: "Well, Mr. Hunnicutt, as I say, I don't know right off if you will have to go to court or not. Sometimes, if a witness tells the truth and one of the parties involved in the dispute knows that their claim doesn't stand a chance, it never goes to court. And most claims don't go to court—they settle out or get dismissed. When someone like yourself sees what happened and has the guts to tell the truth about it, the case often ends right then and there."

HUNNICUTT: "I understand all of that. And I understand that you're just a-doing your job. But do you know what my job is?"

BLK: "Uh, nosir, I do not."

HUNNICUTT: "I didn't think so. Damn lawyers don't know nothin' about what real people have to do to make a livin'. Try to call one of them sonsabitches [sic] about something you need done in a hurry, and you might as well be hollerin' at a barn door to shut after you. They . . . [inaudible, coughing]"

BLK: "Yessir, lawyers can be—"

HUNNICUTT: "—but when it's *you* they need—here they come a-runnin'. They got their gophers like you a-callin' me on the telephone, aggravatin' me

[sic] for weeks about this or that. And if that don't beat it dead, here they come, lickety-split to my house like it's on fire, wantin' me to help them. Then they'll drag a body down to the courthouse, where I'll lose another day or so while the two lawyers jaw at each other some more. And you don't stand the chance of a treed coon under a full moon when you get up on that stand to testify. La mercy, they'll twist your words and trip you up with their smiley-faced questions! That's as true as God's grass is green—I've seen it with my own eyes. They'll turn you into Judas Iscariot himself before you know it. And I won't stand for it. Nosir, the man who wants to come shame me down—that man ought to know I'm a better shot with a raffle [sic – rifle?] than any man in this end of the county—and I can kill a 'coon of a night just as well as I can a buck of a day."

BKL: "Mr. Hunnicutt—please let me explain. No one is trying to make you do or say anything. No one is talking about you going to court. I am just try-ing to talk to you about the dog fight for maybe fifteen minutes. A woman was seriously hurt in this incident, as she was holding on to the smaller dog's leash when the fight occurred. I was told you were a good man who might know some-thing about the dog fight and wouldn't be afraid to tell the truth, so that's why I called."

HUNNICUTT: "Son—I'll tell you this just one more time: I'm not afraid of *anything* or *anybody*! If the High Sheriff himself says I got to go to court, I'll go . . . but you and anyone else will have to get papers on me to say anything more about it."

BLK: "Well, okay. I understand. But let me just tell you this, Mr. Hunnicutt: there's no lawsuit filed about this matter yet. There are no papers to serve. This is just the beginning of things, and I'm just trying to find out what happened . . ."

HUNNICUTT: "Did you talk to Sue Ellen Coates? Wasn't it her what-you-call-it dog—aw, I disremember the name—one of them dogs that looks like the end of a mop. Wasn't it her dog that got kilt [sic]?"

BLK: "Yessir, it was. But I haven't talked to her. "

HUNNICUTT: "Well la [sic] mighty! That beats all! You best go talk to her before you talk to *me!*"

BLK: "But I already know what she has to say about it. She was the one injured and the one who made the claim about the incident."

HUNNICUTT: "Then what in hell do you need me for?"

BLK: "Because there is a dispute about just how the dogfight got started. And in the beginning of our conversation, I thought you said you knew all about it?"

HUNNICUTT: "I do. I'm not telling you different now. But there's no reason to go getting a lot of folks all knotted up with each other about something nobody could have done nothing about nohow [sic]. That little mop dog got kilt [sic] off his own property, and that woman a-walking with him at the time is the first, last, and only person you need to talk to."

BLK: "Yessir, I understand what you mean. But I already know what Missus Coates has said about it, because she is the one making the claim against Ermil Briggs–Coates claims that it was Briggs' Rottweiler that killed her Llasa Apso and subsequently caused her to fall and break her hip. According to my preliminary investigation, there are at least three Rottweilers in that area. But as of yet, I don't have any *other* eyewitnesses who can say how it happened, or which Rottweiler it was. I am hoping you can do that for me, sir."

HUNNICUTT: "No, no, I won't be no help to you a-tall. Ermil Briggs and I go all the way to the back of beyond. I'd trust him with my life. Whatever he says is the gospel truth. If Ermil Briggs tells you something, you can put in the bank and borry [sic - borrow?] from it, it's that good. I'll not contrary him."

BLK: "Yessir, I am sure he's a good man. But I've talked to Mr. Briggs and he says he didn't know anything about it, and he said you might because you were working near his place that day and might have seen what happened."

HUNNICUTT: "Well . . .he's right . . . [clears throat] . . I was [coughs, inaudible] pasturing [sic] my cattle on his land this spring, and I was up there mendin' fence. But I didn't see nothin', didn't hear nothin'. So I can't help you nohow [sic]. Good talkin' to you."

[End of telephone interview with Dwayne Hunnicutt]

Chapter Six

Mayhem in Mayberry: Navigating the NC Court System

I worked both sides of the civil court fence, providing litigation support investigations to both plaintiff and defense-oriented law firms. I also worked directly with corporate HR managers, SIU (Special Investigative Unit) supervisors with insurance companies, criminal defense attorneys—and private pays if they caught me at a weak moment.

Virtually all investigative efforts require due diligence. For me, all due diligence began at the county courthouse. In spite of the pervasive rendering of public records into electronic databases, I insisted on reading the original documents. I had to touch them, sniff them, turn them over to see what might be handwritten on the back, to search them for anything else the digital scanner or data transcriber failed to pick up. I also believed that somehow by just visiting the county courthouse, I derived an understanding of my subject's world that was greater than the sum of the actual records retrieved and reviewed.

Encounters with courthouses in the WNC area were often migraine-inducing ordeals. Despite my experience with legal documents, I was often overwhelmed right at the start of an investigation by the idiosyncrasies of each individual county's records departments.

The majority of due diligence efforts started with the land records maintained by the Registers of Deeds. These were powerful fiefdoms controlled by political patronage, riddled with Machiavellian intrigues and finicky photocopiers, patrolled by formidable women who knew everything going on in their county except what a stranger like me was looking for in *their* courthouse (and they would find that out, too, or perish in the attempt). Their records contained births, deaths, marriages; real property ownership, conveyances and mortgages; personal name changes; military discharges; power of attorney filings.

Next I searched through the civil and criminal records maintained by the clerk and deputy clerks of court under the auspices of the state's Administrative Office of Courts. Here was the really juicy stuff: lawsuits, domestic protective orders, child support enforcements, evictions, liens, judgments, IRS levies, special proceedings files, criminal histories and pending criminal actions.

Then there was the Estates & Probate division to contend with, the repository of wills, death decrees and the subsequent disposition of the decedent's worldly assets.

State and county governments controlled access to and use of these records in accordance with the state's overarching Sunshine Law as set out within N.C.G.S. § 132 regarding the availability of public records. In actuality, however, my access to these records was wholly contingent upon the competence, mood, caffeine intake, and proximity to lunch and quitting times of the deputy clerks and their assistants. Consequently, I had to readjust my expectations of a discreet and efficient records review for every case.

Some courthouses were bright and spacious institutions imbued with the understated intensity of a college library. Others were poorly lit, induced claustrophobia, and forced you to feel the pain of small mountain counties strapped for resources and struggling with the chaotic growth of land transactions, lawsuits, and criminal cases. The resulting chaos was reflected by files spilling over into window frames, files bursting out of musty drawers and rusty cabinets, files buried inside packing boxes stacked in precarious columns along dank basement hallways.

There were courthouses as quaint and trusting as mythical Mayberry. I could wander in and go to work unhindered just as Otis could go lock himself up in Sheriff Taylor's jail. Then there were those tense, hypervigilant dens of constant inquisition wherein my very presence seemed to be an affront, as if I had just barged naked into a family's living room during Easter supper and asked if I could rummage through their dirty underwear.

There were courthouses with imposing grandeur and picturesque landscaping. There were those with their respective courts and records offices hodge-podged together and strung out along several block-long red brick warehouse-type structures called annexes, the structures indistinguishable from the aging textile mills that surrounded them.

The Cherokee County courthouse in Murphy had a gorgeous checkerboard marble floor and soaring rotunda, both of which magnified one's professional ego and one's voice—you had to be careful what you said on the main floor. The Buncombe County courthouse in Asheville postured its somber, neo-classical conservatism in stark contrast to the Art Deco pizzazz of the City of Asheville government building standing right next to it. The two buildings symbolically represent Asheville's bipolar personality, the extremes of which were only hinted at by the county's motto "People to Match Our Mountains." Yet its record rooms were magnificently run and organized. Madison County's intrepid little structure huddled against a stone cliff on one side and peered out over the French Broad River on the other, like it was trying to hide, and maybe for good reason, because the courthouse had been torched in the past by disgruntled litigants. Yet it continued to re-emerge, phoenix-like, from its own ashes. Jackson County's original courthouse stood atop a steep hill in the factory town of Sylva, still dignified although no longer charged with the responsibility of housing county's records and courts of law. In the past I enjoyed sitting in the big courtroom there and intimidating witnesses with my best scowl while hiding in plain sight from the judge by sitting in one of the old wooden seats placed directly behind the naked steel I-beams that supported the ceiling.

All the courthouses in western North Carolina sounded the same, filled with the soft patter of gossip, the crash of heavy metal-backed record books on tables, the whirl and click of microfilm machines, the squawk of printers and the hum of photocopiers. All these courthouses evoked the same conflicting emotions: the sorrow of files "missing" after traveling three hours to review them; the bittersweetness of files miraculously "found" after saying something complimentary about family photos displayed on a clerk's crowded desk; the thrill of speed-reading files to avoid the probing eyes of nosy clerks who kept walking by, simpering falsely while they trolled for clues with "What you looking for, Hon?" or "Who you working for?", or the most common and dangerously ambiguous "Can I help you?"

"Can I help you?" was the most complicated Southernism I had to wrestle with every day. The phrase's intent and meaning could vary tremendously, sometimes in accord with the tone and volume of its delivery, sometimes not. You'd have to be thick as a brick not to marvel at how this simple phrase could embrace so many antithetical and mutually exclusive implications. "Can I help you?" or as it might normally sound, "Kin I HEP you?" encompassed all of the following:

You look kinda lost and a little stupid, like my husband does in the kitchen, so I'll come to your rescue.

You look like a typical rude hasty Yankee man comin' in here messin' up my files, and you'll be pesterin' me sooner or later, so I'll get into this now and get the upper hand of it.

Oh la! Ain't you purty! Hon-ey, why don't you come home with me for lunch and let me fix you some biscuits?"

Outside of the context of a courthouse, the ramifications of "Can I Help You?" could be even more problematic. It could mean *We don't like your kind* or *What the hell are you doing?* or *If you're looking for trouble, it's no trouble for me to give it to you.* If you were on someone's land when you heard *"Can I help you with something?"* you just heard the cocking of a verbal gun, and it might be the last polite request you would ever hear.

Historians and linguists and down-home cultural critics have strip-mined the South's rich rhetorical legacy and storytelling traditions for decades; I cannot hope to match their efforts. I do not fool myself about my Southern credentials. While it is true that I have lived in the South more or less continuously for thirty-two years, and that for the past two decades I have been playing professional hide-n-seek games with native mountain folk, the stark facts remain: I am not now, nor will I ever be mistaken *for* a true Southerner *by* true Southerners.

And rightly so, because I am not a native Southerner.

I was a Rustbelt refugee cut adrift in the Florida sticks at age thirteen. My father, a contractor and superb stonemason, had wanted a better life for us. He made damn sure none of his kids would ever pick up a trowel to make a living. Like other lost children of tradesmen, I sought solutions that were more complicated than the problems they were meant to solve. Needing to escape Florida's drug-addled tourist culture, I hurled myself into academia—which proved to be an even more alienating environment than the one I had just fled. Professors regarded me as an oddity, if at all; campus life was ruled by frat boys whose malice and duplicity seemed to increase tenfold during the Reagan Years. Bitter and beyond broke, I knew I had reached the limits of my poverty and defiance when I found myself using a fishing pole to hook some spare ribs off of a frat rat's barbecue. I left grad school and became an asset analyst for the powerhouse law firm of Vinson and Elkins. Only two years later, I had burned out on the fluorescent-lit anxiety wheel of corporate due diligence work and fled Houston for the beautiful mountains of North Carolina.

Like many idealistic people young and old, I came to the mountains in 1988 to live out the dream of simple living and creative self-reliance—a dream my wife Linda and I have realized over time. But like an old woolen sweater that has suffered too much heat and rain and agitation, the dream seems to fit us much differently now.

Decent jobs with steady pay were hard to find in the Asheville area back in the '80s, and land prices were running away from our reach. We bought a small farm on land "as steep as a mule's face," as they say around here. Our goal was to pay it off in little more than a decade, and to that end we both worked full-time jobs while growing our own organic vegetables, raising lambs for meat and high-quality wool production, using mules to drag down the firewood that heated our old—and uninsulated—farmhouse.

I worked as a paralegal for the Van Winkle Law Firm for eight years, where my in-house investigative responsibilities were virtually the same as those for a private investigator except: 1) I did not require a state license to perform those investigations; 2) I did not have to buy my own equipment and my own liability insurance; 3) I could only provide investigations for Van Winkle attorneys; and 4) I had to water the office Christmas tree and carry office furniture.

Locked inside an office environment, my hyperactive energy would turn dangerously inward. I would run the halls and climb the walls and kick the cubicles of my peculiar confinement, seeking desperately for an honorable way up—or out.

In 1996, the way out was to become a private investigator.

Chapter Seven

Am I Actually a Female P.I.?
The Undercover Debate Continues

The first year that I was out on my own as a P.I., I celebrated every day that I didn't have to deal with office bullshit and wear the asphyxiating tie and confining jacket and the one-size-hurts-all dress shoes. Of course, there were times when I gained certain tactical advantages by looking official. I would wear a suit and tie, have my wife pin my long hair underneath itself, and accept the passing ordeal as sort of a reverse Halloween ritual in which I donned a conservative disguise so as *not* to frighten others.

Most people fantasize about the undercover roles a P.I. can play. In the beginning, I had these same fantasies. But within the first year or two, I learned that the opportunities to go completely undercover were few, indeed. Besides, since P.I.'s do not wear uniforms, the term "undercover" is largely irrelevant, anyway. In general, a true undercover assignment would require you to make continuous, long-term representations of your identity or livelihood as being someone or something other than a P.I. in order to obtain information. Regarding representations of one's livelihood, however, many P.I.'s are marginally employed as such, and must make do with sidelines. So in that sense I guess we *are* undercover much of the time.

I actually achieved my best results being up front with people who knew who I was and what I was doing when I talked with them. To this day I still don't know why folks chose to tell me the things they wouldn't tell anyone else. But they did.

Over the years I worked a wide range of undercover cases: corporate loss prevention operations (i.e., identifying individuals who steal finished goods, machinery, tools, or materials from manufacturers or distributors); premise liability claims (slips and falls); nursing home abuse; trademark infringement cases; missing children and runaway teens; police misconduct investigations; violations of non-compete clauses and other breech of covenant type actions pursuant to business lawsuits; adventure sports liability claims (e.g., horseback riding, mountain biking, whitewater rafting).

While I did not introduce myself as a P.I. for those assignments, my name was my real name for virtually all of them. I wore no disguises. I looked and acted like myself. Since I did not talk about my job with my friends and neighbors, and since I have never advertised my services in the phone book nor really needed to since I worked primarily for attorneys via their word of mouth—there were few red flags to be found. Until the need arose a few years ago for a personal website—and before Google searches became so reflexive in people's everyday lives—I remained relatively unknown.

In many ways, though, I have been undercover all my life.

For starters, there was my Mom's influence. She was our family's original undercover agent. She had a Ferrari brain that was mistakenly installed inside a family stationwagon and then parked in the family garage for far too long. Her mind could be a shooting star, her verbal reflexes superb. She could float like a butterfly, sting like a bee, and still have a delicious dinner for a family of six ready on time. During another era, given other options, her mind might have found its fullest expression as a scholar, a suffragette, a criminal defense attorney, a mad scientist, a hardware store owner, a weblogger featuring the most detailed and convincing conspiracy theories on the Internet.

She had so many contrary and mercurial qualities combined. I spent my entire life trying to understand her. In so doing, I came to be interested in literature, history, politics, murder mysteries, and even wacky *National Enquirer* articles—you know, just Mom stuff.

I can thank my Mom for my predisposition to act at times like some kind of crazed squirrel, racing around to store up enough nuts of sensory data, past wisdom, ancient myths, current events and trivia as a hedge against uncertainty.

And I thank my Mom for her part in making me an identical twin, too.

My opportunities for mistaken identity were plentiful right out of the box, so to speak, and they have lasted for decades. Moreover, I still suffer from many behavioral tics that are often associated with twins. For example, I have the instinctive urge to blend in with whatever emotional and conversational context in which I find myself. I also have the ability to simultaneously talk and listen at the same time, a feat my schoolteachers had dismissed as impossible. But I can talk with someone and yet never miss anything anyone else said within earshot.

This ability is derivative of yet another twin trait—"Twinspeak." Twinspeak is characterized by a fractured, warp-speed syntax—a verbal shorthand, if you will—that compels me to skip over troublesome pronunciations and drop articles and other burdensome grammar in order to convey the most information in the least amount of time. Paired with my twin, I will talk over his words and he mine, the two of us finishing each other's incomplete sentences. To the uninitiated, Twinspeak sounds like mere gibberish or like computer modems conversing. But whenever I am really excited about something or feel the need to communicate imperatives—Twinspeak emerges. That is why I have to transcribe all of my own dictated field notes. Who else but me (or my twin) could make complete sense of the following?

"Subject Braves brown short/blue in/out rez 09:30 09:50 backpack laundry out 10:50 black F150 Fear This south 19-23 gray doublewide 135 Aiken pickup W/F 20's Shady Brady pink tank blue 5-4, 5-5 Shania"

(Translation: Subject wearing brown short-sleeved shirt, blue jeans, and an Atlanta Braves baseball cap entered his residence at 09:30 and again at 09:50 hrs, respectively, removing first a backpack and then a basket filled with loose clothing, both of which he loaded into a black Ford F150 pickup bearing a hood-mounted wind deflector bearing the logo "FEAR THIS." At 10:50 hrs, subject left his residence and proceeded south on US 19-23, turned off on Aiken Road and pulled into a driveway in front of a gray double-wide mobile home located at 135 Aiken Road. A white female, approximately in her twenties, emerged from the trailer wearing a Shady Brady cowboy hat, pink tank top and blue jeans. Female subject appeared to be 5' 4" to 5'5," with a slender build, possibly dyed reddish-brown hair that is thin and cut just below her shoulders; female subject resembled country star Shania Twain).

Then there is my seemingly preternatural gift for resembling other people without any conscious effort to alter my appearance. This ability has not always been a positive aspect of either my personal or professional life. Even close friends will saunter right by me on the street, then draw up with a startled realization: "Oh, it's you. You always look so *different* every time I see you!"

I don't understand it. Once this whole mistaken identity thing caused me to be assaulted by a Volvo stationwagon and a gang of preteen girls right in downtown Asheville. There I was, walking down Walnut Street when this stationwagon swerved over into the oncoming lane, jumped the curb and stopped midway on the sidewalk.

I jumped out of the way but then a pack of little girls poured out of the vehicle and surrounded me. They were screaming over and over in unison and pointing their fingers at me: "YOU'RE PATRICK SWAYZE!" People passing by on the street stopped and looked quite concerned, uncertain about what they were witnessing, as indeed so was I. Because when a Volvo stationwagon pins you against a building and a tiny mob of young girls points their fingers at you and screams something that sounds a lot like "YOU'RE PRETTY CRAZY"—well, it could mean anything, none of it good. An awkward eternal moment ensued before the little girls piled back inside the Volvo and a smiling Mom drove them away, leaving me stunned and staring wordlessly at the larger crowd now staring back at me.

Patrick Swayze had been in the Lake Lure area filming *Dirty Dancing* a year before I moved to North Carolina. I resemble him as much as I resembled the Volvo.

Even more vexing, I have been mistaken for a female private investigator *by* female private investigators with whom I corresponded via email or online professional chat groups. These mix-ups occurred without any intention whatsoever on my part to deceive, and despite the presence of my name and P.I. license number on my signature line. Maybe it's the verbal chameleon-thing. Maybe I use too many adjectives to be a "real" man, hell, I don't know. It just gets weird sometimes.

My investigative approach was more characteristic of female investigators than male, and particularly so of those women without backgrounds in law enforcement. Like them, I had to take investigations to the public without any sovereign immunity for my misdeeds, without a network of firepower and a fleet of vehicles to backup any encounters that go awry. I had learned how to listen to body language and voice inflections as well as they do; to watch and to anticipate which way a conversation was going and gently steer clear of any abrupt obstacles or dead-ends. I had accepted that physical or verbal intimidation would work against an investigator in court, especially a man. That was not cowardice or "going soft" on my part but prudence. "Bad faith" claims—claims filed by the insured against their insurers for alleged outrageous conduct, intentional infliction of emotional distress, defamation, or malicious prosecution—are all too easy to pin on an overtly-aggressive investigator, and if the plaintiff prevails, they are entitled to treble damages.

Female investigators generally tended to over-research their cases in order to avoid confrontations—and errors—at all costs, and this I also did in spades. And when confrontations were unavoidable, I did not rely on intimidation to end them. I preferred to let people take their own time in getting to the subject at hand. I didn't rush them and I didn't push them towards conclusions they weren't already inclined to make. I never pretended to know more about a subject than I did, and my interest in people's stories—howsoever removed from the truth they might have been— was genuine.

Speaking of less than truthful stories, I did not like lies or liars. But lying was a very touchy subject for professionals who were charged with obtaining verifiable and convincing evidence of the most sensitive kind.

P.I.'s actually had very few opportunities for the legitimate use of lies. We bore a considerable legal, ethical, and financial burden of obtaining evidence in a manner that would stand up in court. Outside the context of law enforcement, and utilized by individuals who are not sworn law enforcement officers, lying in order to obtain legal evidence would generally taint you and your evidence.

"Never risk a lot for a little" was the motto for a prudent investigator. There were so many pitfalls to lying on the job: numerous legal precedents that narrowly construed the admissibility of evidence obtained *sub rosa* or through trickery; a myriad of state and federal court rules governing how and what kind of evidence can be obtained and admitted for court; formidable federal laws against pretexting banks and financial institutions for information, against intercepting electronic communications, against conducting third party investigations without the subject's consent that may generate a consumer report that could compromise someone's job or credit history. Pretexting refers to obtaining confidential personal or financial information by impersonating an individual who has a right to know this information, e.g., finance officers, insurance agents; utility service workers, health professionals, etc. Pretexting individuals was often considered unethical by many state bar associations. There was growing popular support to add pretexting to the list of intrusive or negligent behaviors ascribed to P.I.'s and information brokers and consequently outlaw such behavior with so-called privacy laws.

Having said all of that, P.I.'s lied like rugs every day.

The more trustworthy of us preferred to think of ourselves as some kind of amphibious creature who only dwelled part-time in the gray area of confused associations, mistaken first impressions, smooth doubletalk—but who eventually emerged in the light of day with court orders and an attorney's blessing to go out and find the truth.

But we were liars all the same.

And we better be damned good ones, too, because our livelihood, if not our lives, depended upon us fooling frauds, pedophiles, stalkers, drug dealers, con artists, and other professional liars. With dry eyes we peeled the onion of truth layer by layer, lie by lie.

But it didn't stop there. P.I.'s lied to each other about their success so that they would be entrusted with trade secrets and personal confidences. Every day we lied to ourselves that we truly made a difference, that we were infallible, indefatigable, irreplaceable, indispensable assets in the pursuit of truth, justice, and The American Way.

Day after day, year after year, I felt the growing weight of all the ruses, gimmicks, half-truths, bullshit. It accrued like layers of sediment in a drainpipe. The flow of new ideas and true insight got clogged. My identity slowly became a black, furry, foul-looking thing, scary to look at and difficult to deal with.

My earlier fantasies of being undercover had come full circle.

At times, I did not recognize myself.

Chapter Eight

Tacky Tourists: My First
Undercover Assignment

"OH, GOD . . . I'M GOING TO DIE ON TOP OF SOME FUCK-ING FAKE BEAR!"

That was not me.

That was my wife who said that.

The epitome of grace under pressure and the modest owner of the longest emotional fuse of anyone I've ever known, Linda wouldn't reach for an obscenity, let alone the F-bomb, unless something had gone *seriously* wrong during my very first professional undercover assignment.

And dangling precariously some fifty feet above a deformed concrete bear seemed, to her, to be just that.

A client had called me and described an accident that had occurred at Ghost Town in the Sky, a theme park located on a mountaintop that overlooked the lush Maggie Valley in Haywood County. A child had been seriously injured while unloading from a chairlift. The client's premise liability investigation had taken place there during the previous Labor Day weekend—and had failed miserably. Two disposable cameras were the primary suspects in that failure. The client wanted me to perform a discreet investigation of the entire chairlift operation run by the theme park: the pickup and drop-off platforms, the lift operators, the torn carpeting, any and all signs of poor supervision and maintenance that would indicate negligence on the part of the amusement park. He needed the results in one week. He would pay me half of the retainer up front, the rest upon completion of the investigation.

I babbled sympathetically in reply, and uttered the standard assurances peculiar to the legal field: he had my utmost dedication, discretion and thoroughness, yet no guarantee of favorable outcome. Then I quickly hung up the phone.

I leaned back in my chair and closed my eyes and ground my fists into them. I was at sea with my thoughts and feelings. My excitement about my first big undercover assignment was tempered by my misgivings about my client and the loosey-goosey hiring arrangement.

I played the imagined details of the accident in my mind like a mini-horror movie, as I have done with every single accident I've ever heard of in my life. I saw the brightly-colored sneaker entrapped by the worn carpeting. The little body smashed onto the platform and then dragged toward the remorseless gears. The panic, the screams, the chaos. I also imagined my client's forty-eight worthless photos containing other people's intrusive backs, huge blurry faces, blocky legs, looming baby strollers—all the usual suspects that interfere when you try to conduct a premise liability investigation in a crowded environment, let alone on the busiest weekend of the year for such theme parks.

But I had a more pressing problem: I would definitely need a partner on this case. I needed a backup, needed someone to run interference for me while I, the erstwhile innocuous tourist, snapped photo after photo of things not even a deranged tourist would waste their time photographing.

But I could not afford such a partner.

The investigative retainer would barely cover expenses and my "I'm starving for work" low hourly rate. My travel time—just under three hours—would be *pro bono*. So, too, would be the due diligence effort conducted at the Haywood County courthouse prior to ever stepping one cautious but hopefully nonchalant foot into Ghost Town.

Of course, there was the time-honored option of impressing my wife into the service of my business career, but the terms of my professional licensure very clearly prohibited the use of unlicensed investigators or associates to assist in obtaining evidence. I was just starting out, and did not want to run afoul of my licensing board. More to the point, I promised myself when I first received my P.I. license that I would not involve Linda directly in this business. True, she would be the perfect eye magnet, distracting and/or charming all who moved within her sphere. But she was far too perceptive to try to leave in the dark about my mission. She could unwittingly compromise my façade of picture-happy tourist by quite rightly demanding to know just what the hell was I doing taking photos of the grounds and machinery and employees and so forth.

I didn't want to do something technically in violation of my licensure that could lead to my evidence being challenged or barred from the court on down the road—and ultimately to the suspension of my license. And I didn't want to be in the unenviable position of sweating the scrutiny of theme park employees and spouse, alike, as I clicked away with my camera, smiling falsely like a grand piano all the while.

I worried and stewed over this dilemma until I received the retainer via Fed Ex the next day. That settled it. I wasn't about to let the victim down a second time around. So with a mounting sense of doom, I confronted Linda.

"I have to go to Waynesville this Friday to do some courthouse stuff. Do you want to come with me on your day off? You've never seen Waynesville, you could just walk around the downtown area for an hour or so, look at all the antique shops and things—I think they have a bookstore—and then (now speaking softly and rapidly with telling guilt). . . *we-could-go-to-Ghost-Town-in-the-Sky -it-is-supposed-to-be-a-kind-of-corny-themepark-but-very-beautiful-you-can-see-all-of-Maggie-Valley-and-the-Smoky-Mountains-from there.*"

Now I must advise here that I cannot even surprise my wife with good news—birthday gifts and Christmas presents—let alone with bad. Her psychic powers are too great, and my ability to dissemble before her too poor. So naturally, she replied:

"Are we going to Ghost Town to work one of your cases?"

"NO! Uh-uh. I just heard that it was a hoot, you know, like riding the Tweetsie Railroad, one of the obligatory silly things you have to do when you live in this area."

Her calm, clear-eyed gaze first contemplated the bogus me—she knew how I felt about theme parks. Then, she contemplated my bogus justification—she also knew that I was highly allergic to obligatory acts, silly or not. Finally, she decided that assigning a priority to which one was the most bogus at the time wasn't worth the effort. She was game for another Brian Adventure, and perhaps the details didn't matter.

"Okay, it's supposed to be pretty tomorrow. It could be fun."

* * * * * *

"OHH! NOW THE WIND IS BLOWING! GREAT! JUST GREAT!"

"WHY DIDN'T YOU TELL ME WE HAD TO TAKE A CHAIRLIFT?"

Well, I didn't tell her about a lot of things that day. One of the first little details I suppressed about our adventure was that the only other way into Ghost Town besides riding a chairlift was to take the "incline railway," a little tram with open cars in which a young girl had recently disturbed a rattlesnake that had been taking a nap on one of the car seats. The result was predictable, and set out in a lawsuit that I reviewed during that morning's due diligence search at the Haywood County courthouse.

In the Balsam Mountains and throughout Maggie Valley, poisonous snakes are still plentiful, but snakebites are rare. But if they are going to happen at all, the months of September and April offer the unwary some of the best opportunities to get nailed by a sunning rattlesnake.

It was September.

And tourists and theme park visitors and trusting spouses of sneaky private investigators were essentially unwary.

I should add, here, that I have never skied, nor had I previously ridden a chairlift. On the other hand, my wife was a skier. She had ridden on these things before. Just not on one that let out a shuddering groan and jerked to a stop somewhere in the middle of a 3,000 foot ascent and right above a preposterous black bear.

Looking back on it now, I think the bear was the most vexing aspect to our uncertain state of suspended animation. We would both come to regard it as a portend of the desperate tourist schlock— of the surreally bad entertainment experience—that lay waiting for us another thousand feet up the mountain.

The bear was clearly insane: lumpy black body, wild goggle eyes, picket fence teeth and bright red lips. More than likely, it had lost its concrete mind from watching the procession of butts, crotches, legs and feet passing over its misshapen head. Its stupid leer resembled the obscene caricatures of Negroid features found on the old Bull Durham tobacco advertisements. All that was missing was a wedge of watermelon in its cement paws and a text banner fluttering from its grinning maw: "My-My. Lawdy Lawdy. It sho' am good tastin'!" The villainous bruin offended so profoundly that it was justly tattooed with gobs of birdshit, chewing gum, dried ice cream, and phlegm.

"WE PAID $18 BUCKS APIECE. . . FOR THIS?!"

"HOW WILL THEY GET US DOWN FROM HERE?!"

Linda is an unspeakably brave person. But she was just overwhelmed by it all. Dangerous machinery is an anathema to her gentle soul; she also abhors the shoddy, the ramshackle, and the shameless lack of pride in craft. The thought of her young hopeful life ending in a crumpled heap on top of racist country kitsch statuary was just too much for her to . . . bear.

At first, though, we were giddy with the gorgeous day and the truly breathtaking, panoramic view the chairlift afforded. We were soaring through a brilliant sky, over the dusky green humps of forested hills and the mosaic of pastures and cropland that lay mottled under passing puffs of clouds. We soared higher and higher above the diamond flashes of the sun reflecting off of tin roofs and windows below us.

Actually, now that I think about it, we didn't actually soar at all.

We kind of . . . *dangled* . . . progressively up the steep slope.

More specifically, we swung back and forth and somewhat side to side and flopped up and down in the pinched bite of the cable linkage, as if we were something hanging out of a running dog's mouth. And all along, there had been this ominous grinding and occasional clunking that made the chairlift bounce and

Linda gasp and me chuckle appreciatively, monstrous fraud that I was.

But still, there was the unquestionable exhilaration of hanging suspended hundreds of feet over the valley floor and above Jonathan Creek that slithered unseen below us somewhere. Alarmed by the lift's erratic behavior, I attempted to distract Linda with my own, summoning all the boyish bravado I could muster. I swung my feet and pretended to slip out of the seat. I yodeled and yelled out "HEIDI! HEIDI!" and belted out a falsetto Julie Andrews: "*The hills are a-live . . . with the sound of cheap-o chair-lifts.*" I pointed out various mountain peaks to her: there's Cold Mountain to the south; there's the Balsam Mountains and Big Cataloochee Mountain brooding immediately to the north. The Great Smokies were blue-gray waves billowing in the northwest, with Mt. Leconte (6,593 ft), Clingman's Dome (6,642 ft) and Mt. Guyot (6,621 ft)—three of the highest peaks in the Smokies—appearing within our elevated grasp.

It was a hoot.

Until the damn thing crapped out right above the stupid bear.

"I BET YOU KNEW THIS PLACE WOULD BE SO CHEESEY!"

But I really didn't know much about it until that morning. And that bothered me, professionally as well as personally. My due diligence was limited by time, money, and circumstances. I had neither the time nor money with which to search newspapers and other publications for prior incidents at the theme park. There just were not many discreet approaches for the due diligence on this place, period. It was the mid-1990's. Google hadn't appeared yet, and Lexis-Nexis and other database searches were beyond my reach. So I would just have to settle on what I found at the courthouse that morning—and on what I would discover inside the park, as well.

This was my first real undercover assignment, and I was working behind someone else's failure—these facts kept rearing their ugly bear heads. The last thing I wanted to do was to push the Very Small World Theory to its limits and consequently risk compromising this investigation by talking to anyone about this place.

I was familiar with the tourism beast spawned by the Great Smoky Mountains National Park. The body straddled Tennessee and North Carolina; its limbs crawled through the torturous highway US 441, working their way up through Gatlinburg, Dollywood, Sevierville, and Pigeon Forge (Tennessee), then down to the Cataloochee ski area, Cherokee Indian Reservation and Maggie Valley (North Carolina). Scattered hither and yon amongst these well-known attractions were hundreds of tourist traps, motels, flea markets, antique shops, seasonal produce stands, factory outlet stores, NASCAR memorabilia kiosks, log cabin rentals, RV camping sites, Harley-Davidson rallies, etc. So prevalent is this commercial litter among the mountain scenery that it is now regarded as the mountain scenery itself.

It made sense to dress and act like an appropriately tacky tourist. I mustn't look or act too approachable, nor too threatening or alarming. I didn't want to spark someone's imagination if they saw me taking photos of, say, a rectangular piece of outdoor carpeting—if indeed it was still in extent. There was no guarantee at all that it would be.

I would never know the full extent of the failure that was the previous investigation. All I knew was that I would never live down my own sense of failure if I didn't do everything humanly possible to prevent it.

I convinced myself that once inside the theme park, I would have to appear to be somebody who could conceivably be interested in chairlift mechanisms. Someone like an idiot (too easy) or an engineer (no way). Or maybe—yes!—someone like a Biker-type dude or Gearhead.

Already possessing tattoos, long hair, a pierced ear, and a ready supply of about a hundred rock concert T-shirts, I chose the Biker-Gearhead look. My faithful and loyal assistant grabbed one of my black T-shirts, as well, probably more out of her fondness for wearing my shirts than as a show of support for her strange husband.

The lift's cable jerked a couple of times, and the single-piece, welded-pipe chair jolted forward, and in some insufferable length of time, we eventually approached the end of the line for the lift.

Several hundred feet before the actual lift landing, there stood a tower that had a little cabin on top of it, like a little forest ranger tower. A huge sign that read "SMILE!" hung just above the cabin window cut-out. Standing inside the cabin were two young women who took a photo of everyone who drooped towards them on the lift, and then sold the photo back to them at double the cost.

I still have that photo. It is one of my all-time favorite photos of us together.

At the moment the photo had been taken, Linda was smiling hugely. I believe that under her forced grin, she was still muttering about the bear. I was beaming cheerfully, as well. To look at us, you'd never guess that I was a duplicitous P.I. sweating my first undercover assignment and that my wife was rather stressed out by our adventure so far.

We looked so happy. We looked so young and healthy and confident . . . like we could do anything, do everything . . . and that some day, we would. We looked ready to roll our strength into one ball and shoot out of the frail confines of the lift chair and hurtle through the azure ceiling above us, upward through the crystalline intermeshed spheres of the cosmos, challenging the very limits of An Unknowable Pinball Universe and making that sucker give us an extra game.

I imagine that my own full-of-myself smile lasted up to the time the chairlift was scudding along the landing platform. Right up until I saw the puckered gash in the green carpet.

And then the sun dimmed to brown and birds stopped singing and livestock quit grazing and dogs all over the world lifted their heads in alertness, sensing the danger. And the ridiculousness of my day disappeared, replaced by a sudden throat-parching, hair-lifting realization that the center of my world might, despite her innate athleticism, step in the exact same carpet hole on the chairlift landing that had snared the child's foot—the very hole that was the focus of this investigation.

The carpet hole lay in the center of an approximately three foot by three foot square that had been delineated by strips of masking tape.

There was also a sign urging lift passengers to step down exactly within the square area marked by the masking tape.

Linda was eager to leave the lift. She was already leaning forward, readying her balance to leap off the chair.

One of the three lift operators—an extremely short, knobby-muscled, bearded man with only one opened eye—stuffed his cigarette back in his mouth and bounded towards her. He thrust one of his work-swollen hands at her. She hesitated, staring at the proffered hand covered in calloused warts, the fingers nicotined orange and bumpy and looking for all the world like strings of tater tots.

He lunged towards her again and gripped Linda's pale slender hand. With a grunt he pulled her up and away from the chair lift and, at last, sent her soaring through the air the way the chair lift never could.

He brought her right down in the middle of the taped area. At the last split-second, her right foot darted to the side and she missed the foot-eating hole by inches.

I jumped off the lift, and heard Linda say something about the hole.

"Did you see that hole? That's dangerous. Someone could get badly hurt. I can't believe they haven't fixed that."

"Yeah, you're right. But aren't these huge flywheels and gears cool, though? I want to take a few pictures of this before we head out to the rides and things."

There's a new cubicle in Hell.

And it has my name on it.

Like Dante's Hell, Ghost Town was configured in varying levels—pain thresholds, if you will—in what was essentially a three-tiered paved parking lot gooped on top of a lovely mountain. You arrived by lift or tram at the lowest level, which features a kiddie park, a shooting gallery, concession booths and retail shops. Next, you either hoofed it, or rode golf carts or minibuses, up to the second level, which featured among its carnival rides the roller coaster aptly named "The Red Devil." Then, you straggled on up to the third or top level to the Wild West theme area, with its scheduled bank robberies, shoot-outs, saloon girls, as well as other attractions and rides.

We couldn't begin to explore the place until I had captured on film the carpet hole and the rest of the risky lift landing. It was still early, well before noon. The crowd was sparse, limited to a dozen or so single adults with their children, a few couples, some foreign tourists. The lighting was excellent if not maybe a little too bright. The park employees appeared focused on their own coffee, cigarettes and conversations.

Time to do it.

We sauntered back towards the lift landing. I struck up a conversation with the little warty one-eyed banty rooster of a lift operator. It wasn't too long before we were joined by another lift operator—a leathery woman with brass-colored hair and bold black eyes—and finally by Linda. The park employees were non-committal at first, but eventually their gruff demeanor seemed to melt away with the sun's increasing strength, and we chatted at length about a wide range of topics. They became cheerful and animated and I soon felt the familiar twinge of remorse about getting chummy with people whose goodwill—and most likely their jobs—would disappear once they learned of the consequences to their friendly conversation with an undercover P.I.

For a good while under the hot sticky September sun, we few, we misfit few, dropped our business faces and just enjoyed bullshitting each other. Together we cursed the unreliability of hangover remedies. We marveled at the irresistible hold that great heights, open valleys, fragile cable lifts, heavy gear mechanisms, and worn carpeting all have on people. We laughed as we shared mountain weather folklore, personal hard luck stories, construction accident anecdotes, drunken mishaps, stupid tourist tricks. We pondered the fickleness of fate, and we all solemnly nodded our heads in agreement . . . *yes, the number of accidents that had occurred at this particular theme park did seem a little high . . . .*

When I confessed my fascination for the lift machinery and my desire to photograph it *repeatedly*, the lift operators seemed to accept and even enjoy my wife's nonchalant yet trenchant assessment:

"He is *so* odd. What can you do?"

They seemed comfortable with whatever altered state of consciousness I was currently exhibiting, and so they smiled indulgently as I photographed the lawsuit-loving landing, and they even posed with Linda and I for gag photos. We bid them goodbye, and they went back to the sweltering tedium of hurling heavy and oblivious people off of lift chairs and keeping darting kids away from the remorseless bite of flywheels, pulleys, and cables. And we went on to tour Ghost Town.

The crowd contained a noticeable contingent of badly dressed, unshaven, gimlet-eyed men who were slouching aimlessly about, exchanging shifty looks, wearing cameras, pointedly examining handholds and stairways and fencing and amusement ride towers, prodding listless children in front of them as they struggled up the inclined walkways or meandered into amusement arcades. My first suspicion was that their presence attested to the sad reality behind divorced dads and their choice of cheapskate entertainment for their estranged children during visitation days. My second suspicion—that the place was crawling with private investigators conducting covert premise liability investigations—did not necessarily rule out the first.

Linda and I hiked up to the Wild West town. We arrived at the end of one of the scheduled shoot-outs. We heard lackluster voices shouting challenges, heard the gunshots, saw the scheduled carnage. We didn't follow the crowd as they left for their next planned diversion, so we watched the dead outlaws springing back to life, brushing the sawdust off their Carhartt-brand jeans and fishing out a new plug of chew from their back pockets. The town Sheriff was a chesty high school graduate and wannabe police officer whose "dream job" of wearing a badge and shooting people with impunity didn't end up quite like he'd planned. He talked to us at length as he downed a well-earned Mountain Dew and fitfully reloaded blanks into his six-gun and adjusted his badge. At the same time, he explained to us the timing of the next shows and urged us, in a rather forlorn tone, not to miss them.

We decided to go visit the town jail instead.

Behind bars were mannequins, costumed dummies who represented someone's idea of the typical scofflaws of the Old West. There was a mustachioed Mexican with eyes closed, crooked and missing teeth bared, wrapped up in his sombrero and colorful blanket. The Mexican appeared to be either sneezing or snoring into perpetuity. Slouching next to the Mexican was a bizarre-looking Native American. Given the proximity of the Cherokee Reservation—and given that the park featured actual young Cherokee dancers who danced artfully, on a concrete floor, several shows a day—perhaps the Indian's tribal allegiance was made deliberately ambiguous. The plaster cast faces on both the Indian and the Mexican looked . . . totally plastered. An empty bottle of Popov Vodka—their firewater of choice—sat open between them, the protestations of their phantom jailers notwithstanding.

There was also a white man in the jail: a "Yankee Slicker" or carpetbagger-type dandy. He sat apart from the drunken Mexican and Indian. This mannequin wore a tall top hat and full coat and tails. His overstuffed valise sat by his hip. His pose was markedly affected, with his body leaning at an angle, legs crossed effeminately high at the thigh, his one arm wafting airily in an exaggerated gesture of dramatic oration or immediate swoon. The pale thin-featured androgynous face was frozen forever in some unknown complaint. Someone had spit on him, and not too recently, either: a dried gob of phlegm hung crusty and green on the end of the dummy's nose. On the dandy's forehead, scrawled plainly in black ink, was the well-intentioned warning to all jail visitors, young and old alike:

"I Give Head."

The rest of the park sucked, too.

In the balance of the things that did and did not happen to us that day, I'd still say the assignment was a success. I got the photos my client needed. We didn't die or suffer any traumatic physical injuries. I didn't get caught and I was never challenged about what I was doing there.

Unfortunately, I never did get paid the remaining half of the retainer owed to me. I learned the hard way about accepting out-of-state assignments. And I did blow the discretion and confidentiality of my first undercover assignment: Linda had figured out rather quickly what was going on. She had suspected all the while, but didn't let on until we had returned to our vehicle.

"Well, that wasn't completely horrible. Pretty views. It's sad that so many people get lured into visiting such a phony, run-down place."

"Yeah, that's true."

She looked right through me with her beautiful eyes so light blue they glimmered silver in the bright sunlight.

"You should have told me you needed me for your investigation, though."

Boned!

"Well—would you have come with me if I had?"

"Of course."

"What if I had told you about the chairlift? What if you had known about the bear . . . and the carny . . . and the Yankee mannequin?"

She shrugged and placed her hand in mine.

"I wouldn't have liked it. But I would have done it for you."

That was the first, last, and only job I ever got to work with the best investigation partner in the world.

Chapter Nine

Cheaters and Beaters Make the World Go Round: Domestic Investigations

When I first became a P.I., I swore I wouldn't do domestic work. I wanted to avoid the hassle of private pays and the even bigger hassle of working for divorce lawyers, who were notorious for begrudging every penny of the investigative retainer and quibbling over every item in an investigator's invoice.

I knew the hours for domestic would be terrible. I knew that in most instances I would have to have a reliable partner for the surveillance part, which would be difficult to find on the usual short notice P.I.'s receive for assignments. I did not want to hire a full-time partner; I could barely coordinate my own schedule, let alone someone else's. Besides, the feast-or-famine nature of P.I. work inevitably created unrealistic expectations and subsequent disappointments for both parties.

Finally, I thought that I would make enough money from personal injury and worker's comp cases to avoid working domestic.

Turned out that I was right about everything but the last one.

Domestic cases were never worth it. But peeping on cheaters and beaters paid the bills. I worked as few as I possibly could. Cynicism and black humor offered no lasting defense against prolonged exposure to marital infidelity. When your busiest days for catching cheaters were Christmas Eve, New Year's Eve, Super Bowl Sunday and Valentine's Day—you became jaded fast.

Even more demoralizing was child custody or "kiddie repo" work, in which you attempt, via surveillance and discreet field interviews, to determine whether the quality of the custodial parent's home life is so egregious in the eyes of the court to overturn custody rights. The children always seemed to lose in the end;

their hearts and minds torn by their parents' nonstop, everywhere, no quarter warfare of reprisal and control, or their bodies by abuse and neglect.

There was way too much client hand-holding that went with domestic assignments. You couldn't bill for all the time you spent keeping folks already frazzled by marital discord from going off the deep end.

As far as I could tell, everyone going through a divorce was temporarily insane. As for the physical and emotional side, it was plain to see that a messy divorce was like having a serious car wreck every day of your life for about three years. Or more like a rodeo in which you were the bull and the rider *and* the clown all at the same time.

For marital infidelity cases, at least a woman client would make it easier for me. She'd know whom I'd be following. Indeed, she would know *everything* about her: her name, where she worked, what perfume she wore, her cell phone number, who her friends were, where she shopped, where she ate, the best time to catch her screwing the client's husband, whether she wore wigs. And when confronted with the moment of truth, the female client would be more of a *man* about the whole thing than the husbands usually were in the same situation. She would present a taut jaw and tightly pressed lips, white lines forming around her mouth and down from the corner of her nose, and a tear or two sliding down a cheek. She would nod her head to herself, then take a sharp sniff before speaking with a slight quiver to her voice—but with complete resolve: "Okay. Okay. I know what I need to do now. Thank you so much."

Thank you. Thank you for proving beyond a reasonable doubt that there is indeed a physical dimension to my otherwise bottomless despair and sense of betrayal. And for proving that dimension actually wears Lady Stetson perfume and a size 6.

The men? Forget it. Way too much trouble, mostly. Oh, you could make a lot of money from them. You could follow their spouse's interactions with dozens of suspects: her supervisors, her co-workers, her old boyfriend who called her a year ago around New Year's Eve, some unknown man who always winked at her in the post office, the entire work crew at Thrifty Muffler, *et al.* You got to use all of your ridiculously expensive high-tech gear—long-range optics, covert cameras, real-time GPS-linked vehicle tracking devices, time-lapse or extended real-time VCR's, infrared spotlights and night-vision goggles—because men loved that stuff, even when it was unnecessary. Sometimes you could even keep your boy from interfering with your otherwise discreet investigation. It really sucked to find out *after* a determined boyfriend poured a gallon of house paint all over my front windshield that my client was a cuckold *and* a blabbermouth. And after awhile, you got used to your male clients calling you around the clock with impossible demands, absurd leads and improbable scenarios, bellowing their outrage, hissing their conspiracies.

But when you confronted them with the evidence of their wife stepping out—

look out! I've been screamed at, barfed on, bear-hugged breathless, and hurled to the ground in a reflexive violent spasm of a wounded heart belonging to a man-moose. I've watched men drive their fist through walls and windows, rip my printed photo summaries to shreds, jerk the VCR out of the wall and smash it on the ground. I've wrestled loaded guns from their hands; I've spent *hours* off the money clock dissuading them from committing acts criminal, acts cruel, or acts mind-numbingly stupid.

Domestic assignments cover more than kiddie repo and cheaters and beaters. I never found joy in any of them. Birth mothers searching for the children they gave up for adoption? Somehow I never got the blissful reunion scenes like those on *Oprah*. You don't know what a real scream sounds like until one erupts from a 20-year-old woman who just found out over the phone that her entire young life was a lie because she was actually adopted and never told.

"Your birth mother would like to get in touch with you; she's concerned that you are nearing child-bearing age and she would like you to know about your genetic history. Do I have your permission for her to have your contact information and get in touch with you?"

"NOOOOOOOOOOOOO!"

Runaway teens? Very challenging. You got to go undercover and hang out at Rainbow Gatherings, drummings, college dorms. But wait until you outfox everyone and bend heaven and earth to locate a runaway, only to return her to a bona fide abusive home. That takes the wind out of your sails.

Finding missing children who were kidnapped by a non-custodial parent? Proving or disproving child sexual abuse? Uncovering institutional child abuse? These were all admirable quests, ones that would incite even the most cold-blooded P.I.'s into freely lavishing their time and resources to help solve these cases.

But female investigators were much more successful in handling the face-to-face requirements of these and other cases involving children. Whatever hard-won triumphs there may have been with these cases were largely theirs alone. My role was usually behind-the-scenes research, such as tracking perpetrators or locating witnesses. Even so, both the protracted agony and dubious outcome of the majority of these cases embittered me to no end. Like a dog that crawled into a bathtub and trembled and howled during a passing thunderstorm, I merely endured these cases anyway I could, and didn't behave very stoically while they were ongoing, either.

Finding missing heirs was kind of fun: an Easter Egg Hunt and Christmas all at once. But usually the vibe was not *Great Expectations* but *Taxi Driver*. If someone had disappeared without a trace for three years or more, more than likely they were dead, in prison, joined a cult, or had very compelling reasons not to be found and thus behaved very badly when they were. No one clever enough or sociopathic enough to hide for years would fall for the old "I've got money for you" ruse, even if it turned out to be true.

No one, that is, except maybe a P.I. "I've got money for you" worked every time for them. Domestic cases proved it.

Chapter Ten

On the Streets of West Asheville:
A Domestic Surveillance Story

There was a young man not a full foot away from me who was staring at his reflection in the van's left passenger window. He started patting at his bleached blonde fade and plucking at his nose and ears—and he didn't see me sitting inside the van, behind normal, lightly tinted auto glass, even though it was bright daylight.

I gloated about this. Even though I knew better than to gloat about anything in this profession.

But I couldn't help it. It was uncanny. He turned his head away from himself in the window and, crouching down, his shoulders hunched forward, faced the driver's side-view mirror. With finger and thumb, he began to mine his nostrils in earnest.

I didn't stare at him directly, because then he would get that funny feeling that he was being stared at—and I didn't want him to have any funny feelings at all. I didn't want him to wonder if there could be anything more to the bronze-colored Soccer Mom-type van that he was presently using as a vanity mirror, and which I was presently using as a surveillance vehicle. I didn't want him to examine every window so closely that he seized upon the significance of the unusual rectangular haze inside the van, a haze that obscured some interior objects yet not others. Because that rectangular haze was actually a special type of very sheer cloth suspended inside the van that acted to break up the outline of things and people hiding inside. With this cloth, it was unnecessary to use the heavily blackened or mirrored window tinting that made most surveillance vehicles so conspicuous.

Uh-oh. Maybe this guy is actually looking for me in here . . . or maybe scoping out the van for a rip-off session. No . . . he's actually another P.I., working the other side of my case . . . and about to have the time of his life burning me at my surveillance site AND making me watch him clean out his nostrils at the same time!

Ah. Turned out, he was just some everyday kind of dude, and he left. He left with a better 'do and a cleaner nose, too. God bless him.

And bless me also. Because I had survived a very close encounter, and that meant my cover was good.

I gloated a bit more.

I had not appreciably changed my physical position inside the van in more than five hours. The arrival of The Nosepicker seemed like a lifetime ago. The painful truth was that I could not change my position. Because if I did, the van would wiggle from the slightest shift of my weight, and the van's radio antenna would waggle to and fro. Such movement would have been a very odd thing for a supposedly empty van to do, especially a Soccer Mom van that had been closed up and parked for five hours on a city street in March. Even here in West Asheville, where unpredictable things happen to the insides and outsides of empty cars all the time, inexplicably fidgety vans were still considered provocative.

I had parked here at 15:00 hrs. My surveillance log had noted The Nosepicker at 16:00 hrs; it was now 20:30. The foil sunshade that I had stuffed on top of the dashboard had helped to keep the low-angled late winter sun from highlighting me, but not from baking me inside the metal skin of the van. I had to keep reminding myself that the hot plastic smell filling the van was actually emanating from the circuitry of my electronic surveillance gear, and not from the van's interior melting all around me. The mesh of my screening cloth was so finely woven that it blocked most of the already limited amount of fresh air that entered the van through two windows lowered ¼ of an inch. I could not run a DC fan or a "Swampy"-type evaporative cooler because my position was just too open. The fan might have fluttered the sheer material of the screen and called attention to it, and the temperature was not hot enough outside to dissipate the cooling fog that a "Swampy" might have exhaled all over the van's windows.

When it got dark, the temperature dropped sharply, back into the low forties and sinking steadily. My sweat had dried inside my black heavy cotton jumpsuit, and I shivered slightly with the arrival of the evening coolness. I was sitting in a semi-sprawled crouch, head hanging low beneath the profile of the seat's headrest. As viewed from the side, this posture would have been familiar to anyone who had ever visited a chiropractor's office and observed the body chart of severe spinal misalignment caused by acute trauma or lifelong neglect.

* * * * * *

A haphazard collection of racially diverse, largely blue-collar urban neighborhoods and businesses, West Asheville can feel warm and inviting one moment, mean and gritty the next. Indeed, it has an unpredictable personality and, in certain neighborhoods, a dangerously schizoid one at that. It has always been regarded as the black sheep kin to downtown Asheville, often acting like the kind of brother who would charm his way into a family reunion, only to get shitfaced, scarf down the food, and then barf all over the kids. After such outrages, the self-appointed promoters of the mellow bohemian spirit and trust-funded eclecticism that imbues downtown Asheville would wail and gnash their capped teeth and pray to Mammon that West Asheville would just . . .take a timeout or something, just *chill!* And when that didn't work, they would send their cops out *en masse* to perform the nasty magic they wanted done, but never wanted to know *how*.

Even today, West Asheville is still the last remaining affordable area within walking, biking, or staggering distance from jobs, stores, schools, bars, and the downtown district. It is struggling to keep its quirky messy compelling self intact, and to just survive, period. But that is what West Asheville—disregarded in the past as "*Worst* Asheville"—has always done, and probably always will be doing. It has wrestled to a draw the sprawling Norfolk/Southern Railroad depot, the labyrinthine tracks of which tie together the remaining heavy fabrication and industrial salvage operations that clutter the banks of the French Broad River, which separates West Asheville from downtown Asheville in more than geography. It has resisted the hostile efficiency promised by the interstate connector I-240 (soon to become I-26) loop that roars through the heart of it, preferring instead that "jump and bump" rhythm provided by the endless 4-way stop signs and stoplights.

West Asheville bears the brunt of the conflicting desires coming from the Buncombe County courthouse and City Hall, Asheville's twin towers of control and commerce. Stay profitable yet neglected. Stay a vibrant, inclusive urban area yet still serve as a catch basin for the city's problems both human and environmental. Stay picturesque and accessible yet remain out of sight when tourists flow through the city, leaking dollars as they go. The city's burgeoning medical care corridor, dominated by the vast Mission-St. Joseph's Hospital complex and its teeming spawn of doctors' parks, invades West Asheville's body from the east, feasting on the marrow of its work hard, play hard ethos. Gentrification is also gnawing through the tough old red brick and corrugated metal of the former factories, warehouses and machine shops, leaving in its wake an overly-contrived funkiness that West Asheville's long-time funky inhabitants can no longer hope to afford. Last but certainly not least, Big Box churches and Bigger Box retailers continue to devour the remaining overgrown vacant lots and other impromptu gathering places, the massive structures looming over the neighborhoods like Norman castles beyond the Pale—and sharing those castles' primary function.

But it is still crazy West Asheville—now sometimes called "Westville" if you're hip or a realtor but never both at the same time. Removed from the context of my usual rural surveillance settings, West Asheville thrilled me every time I had the chance to work there: I was finally "working the streets," as they say, like a "real" P.I. As soon as I crossed the river and began angling my way through the twisted, tree-shrouded streets, I always expected to see a sign somewhere that read: "West Asheville - IT CAN HAPPEN HERE."

* * * * * *

Immobilized for hours, I was in a unique position to experience the diurnal forces at work on this exciting maze of both stately and crooked homes, of both picturesque and sinister streets. I watched children trudge home from school in groups or as solemn singles. I watched men and women carefully park vehicles, flick their cigarette butts out into the street, and hurry towards their homes that popped open and emitted pets and cooking smells and the welcome glow and garble of TV. I marveled at the spontaneous growth of cats atop warm car hoods and tires, or otherwise skittering many-footed past me when a fugitive dog appeared, his broken tether trailing jauntily behind him. The dog trotted up next to my van and suddenly started sniffing my vehicle, circling it twice and whining, his keen attention making my heart beat faster. Then he cocked his leg and unceremoniously appropriated my splattered left front tire into his domain, and hurried off for more acquisitions. He left me alone, another good omen. Another brief gloat occurred.

But what I had not seen so far . . . was any activity at all inside the two-story wood-frame house, painted eggnog with red trim, located at 1155 Hanover, a house that was only about fifty feet in front of me and to the right. A small fluorescent light burned in what appeared to be the kitchen. A tiny red light was flashing from behind a bedroom window, probably coming from an alarm clock or answering machine or some other appliance. A dolphin-shaped wind chime hung mutely from the front porch, revolving ever so slowly in an imperceptible breeze. Otherwise, no activity observed.

My preliminary investigation had suggested that my client's wife would, in all probability, drive her 1994 Volkswagen Jetta home from work, dash into her house for a shower and a change of clothes, and then dash out of the house again and into one of three possible vehicles her boyfriend might own, operate, or simply be a fellow passenger. On my "hotsheet"—what I called my one-page summary of the most vital information required in the field for a given assignment—were all of the relevant vehicle descriptions and NC DMV license tags and correlative vehicle owner information. Some digital still photos I grabbed from a brief video of her walking to her place of work were on the hotsheet as well, for identification purposes. My cell phone had the residence phone number stored for quick dial as a last resort to confirm whether anyone was inside. Yet I knew from previous experience that her answering machine would undoubtedly defeat that line of inquiry.

My client's allegedly wayward wife was now two hours late for her presumed normal return home. I had arrived here two hours earlier than my best guess for her time of arrival, in order to unobtrusively secure a site by the house. I had to park so closely because of the configuration of the neighborhood: houses with extremely short setbacks; houses in close proximity to each other; houses flanked by stout tree trunks, dog fences and ornamental shrubbery; houses with most of the occupants parking their vehicles on the street upon returning home from work. And parking so closely to the subject residence gave me just enough of a window of opportunity to glimpse the fleeting yet critical manner of her ingress and egress from the marital home.

Three seconds. That's the time it would take her to walk from the street to the sidewalk and behind the obscuring trees. Another three seconds and she would be in the house. At some point, she would take another three seconds to leave the house and get to the tree line, and then three seconds more to get into someone's car and be gone.

It took my Sony digital videocamera three seconds to click on and become operational from the off position. It took three seconds to look away to watch a child chase a ball into traffic, three seconds to be distracted by my leg falling asleep, three seconds to slowly realign my wry neck, three seconds to scan my hotsheet, three seconds to grope for my slim black dictaphone which had slipped out of a black jumpsuit pocket and onto the seat somewhere in the dark.

Forget the hundreds of surveillance hours I'd conducted successfully in the past. Forget my five hours of stillness. No matter what I did or didn't do, three seconds would make the difference between me being a hero or a chump.

It took three seconds for my eyes to adjust from an oncoming SUV burning its high beams straight through my brain. The SUV cruised slowly up Hanover. Minutes later, the same SUV drove by again in the opposite direction. A Nissan Pathfinder. I noted the time and the vehicle's tag. There was something familiar about that vehicle. I couldn't place it at the time, though. NC DMV was closed, so I couldn't run the plate.

Is this her? Is it the boyfriend driving, staking out the place first? No drug dealers on this block that I can tell, so the SUV ain't looking to score. Hah! It must be her. I suspected this might be easy, just a few hours due diligence surveillance, nothing too fancy, no need for a second investigator, nothing to drain the surveillance retainer down too far. Just a little night out on the street to confirm the vehicle, confirm the pattern, perhaps if it looks safe to follow loosely, see where they go, maybe get a money shot of a public display of affection . . . or maybe an overnight stay? That would be—

Bzzzzzzzzzzzzz! Bzzzzzzzzzzzzz!

I had conquered my body's instinct to jump with alarm whenever the vibrating cell phone felt like it was sawing off my hipbone. But I was helpless to stop it from flooding me with adrenaline or panicking me with flashbacks to numerous encounters with hornets.

Bzzzzzzzzzzzzz! Bzzzzzzzzzzzzz!

Who. In. The. Hell. Is calling me ?

The cell phone's cover was closed up, so the LED display did not cast a greenish glow inside the darkened vehicle: I could not tell who was calling me. I knew that it could not be a client because I never gave out my cell phone number to clients. Only a handful of P.I.'s had it, because they had worked subcontract for me on surveillance assignments, when cell phones were necessary when we got separated beyond the range of our two-way radios. I forbade them from giving the number out under the dubious threat of never hiring them again if they did.

But I figured the call might be from my wife, so I made sure the phone's earpiece was snug before I answered in a sepulchral whisper:

"Go ahead."

"HEY, BRIAN!? HELLO? BRIAN? HEY, THIS IS KENNY, ARE YOU THERE? ARE YOU THERE? HAS SHE SHOWN UP YET? I DON'T SEE HER JETTA!"

I never ever say my name over the cell phone. But in this surprising instance, I didn't have to. It was my client. He had committed an unpardonable sin: interfering with his own case. Yet he had also performed a miracle of sorts: obtaining my cell phone number. The latter effort was impressive, considering my cell phone account was not in my name to begin with.

My client had transformed himself into a remarkable hybrid creature: half fool, half sharpie. He had piqued my curiosity to the point where I didn't hang up on him instantly.

"Advise if your cell phone is on digital or analog function?"

"ADVERTISE WHAT? IS THIS BRIAN? HOLD ON . . . HAVE TO TURN AROUND HERE."

"Please advise if your cell phone is on digital or analog. Look for "D" or "A" somewhere on your display."

I had wanted to make sure his cell phone wasn't on analog mode, because if it was, this neighborhood was thick with radio frequency scanners that would pick up his communications. I heard the sound of heavy breathing, much thumping and fumbling, and a radio in the background and the honk of a car horn.

"UH – OH – YEAH, IT'S A MOTOROLA, IT SAYS "D"—THAT'S DIGITAL, RIGHT?"

"Yes. Digital is what we want."

"SO WE'RE GOOD TO GO?"

"Acknowledged. What do you want?"

"I WANTED TO KNOW, YOU KNOW, IF YOU GOT HER, IF YOU SAW—"

"Stand By . . ."

The glare of headlights splayed across my vehicle's interior, and I looked up towards the front of the van in order to use the rearview mirror to see what might have been coming behind me. It was the Pathfinder again, with that odd roof rack they have. Making a positive ID of the SUV was difficult, as the vehicle's color and shape seemed to undulate as it flowed through competing pools of light: vehicle lighting, street lighting, residential indoor lighting, security lighting.

Kenny's voice cut into my ear again.

"HEY . . . I'M COMING UP HANOVER RIGHT NOW! WHERE ARE YOU? I'M DRIVING A CHARCOAL PATHFINDER . . . WHERE ARE YOU? FLASH YOUR LIGHTS WHEN I GO BY YOU, OKAY?!"

Unbelievable. No, sadly, it is too believable. No, really, it is too unfuckingbelievable. Sigh.

West Asheville—It Can Happen Here.

"HEY BRI—OOPS . . . SORRY. C'MON, TALK TO ME, DUDE. I NEED TO HEAR SOME GOOD NEWS! YOU SAID WE'RE GOOD TO GO IF I'M DIGITAL, SO WHAT'S UP?"

The mental image of The Nosepicker going "digital" appeared again, adding to my torment. Yet the absurdity of it all helped to dampen down the fires of my increasing irritation. As I watched the Pathfinder crawl by, I viewed with satisfaction the grim white face dodging back and forth, frantically scanning the parked cars.

The driver was Kenny. My confidential client.

"Please leave the area immediately. We'll talk later. If you do not leave, I will terminate this job and our contract. But tell me first . . . how did you get this number?"

"I CALLED THAT OTHER P.I., THE ONE YOU TOLD ME ABOUT WHEN WE FIRST TALKED? SHE GAVE IT TO ME. HEY, YOU'RE REALLY GOOD. I CAN'T SEE YOU AT ALL ANYWHERE!"

Another subcontract P.I. had been struck from the list—and possibly a paying domestic client. Shit.

See what happens when you gloat?

He didn't seem like such a moron when I interviewed him. Hell, I cannot spend all of my free time investigating the intelligence or freak-out factor of every domestic client! Checking them out for criminal backgrounds, violent behavior, concealed weapon permits, financial solvency, and litigiousness is a big enough of bite out of the time pie. I do remember our first meeting . . . he drove the Pathfinder . . . and he kept doodling his wife's name on one of the table tents at the restaurant.

A suspicion flared up in my stomach.

"Acknowledged. Advise if anyone else knows about this matter tonight?"

"UH-UH, NO WAY! I DIDN'T TELL NO ONE . . . NOT EVEN CINDY."

Another gut-level twang of doubt. Followed by a frisson of alarm.

I was undone. Kenny had blown it.

I had been so resourceful, diligent, stealthy, and confident. All for naught. I had been reduced to just another apprehensive lump of humanity cowering motionless inside a rental van and sucking stale surveillance vehicle air while gasping out terse commentary over a cell phone to a hyperactive cuckold.

The transformation had taken. . . . about three seconds.

Not even Cindy.

Or three words.

I scanned the darkened house at 1155 Hanover, noting sourly the empty parking space right in front of the house.

"Acknowledged. Hang up and leave immediately. Do you copy?"

A long exhale and then "OKAY, SORRY, MAN, LISTEN, I DIDN'T MEAN—" *beep.* I terminated the call.

The Pathfinder sped away and grew small in the distance. Kenny was out of here, out of my hair.

It took me several minutes to regain my focus, to check my surroundings for changes, to enter my observations in my audio surveillance log: "*20:35. Client called on cell phone, advised he was in vicinity of surveillance site; observed client driving late model Nissan Pathfinder, NC TAG Nancy Sam Frank 6768-; client drove past marital home and this investigator's surveillance vehicle. Investigator advised client to leave area immediately. Client advised investigator he told no one about surveillance effort—ADVISE suspicion that investigation may have been compromised by client. ADVISE will terminate surveillance at 21:00 hours if no activity observed. . . .*"

My surveillance log ended there. But the tape recording continued. I must have been so distracted by my client's intrusion that I didn't click off my dictaphone, so it just went on recording for quite some time after he had left the scene.

If you were to listen to the tape recording, right in the middle of the long stretch of hissing tape noise that is the inevitable consequence of countless re-recordings—you could hear it happen.

I had several small digital recorders. They were perfect for witness interviews. They had superior audio clarity that does not degrade with re-recording and the recording can be imported into my computer and preserved on computer storage media. Also they have a precise date/time function that helped corroborate the evidence.

Digital recorders were expensive and fragile, however. I didn't use them for mundane tasks in the field such as surveillance logs, drive-by activity reports, mileage/expense reminders, due diligence notes, etc.

So that means that on my beat-up Sony microcassette dictaphone—the one with all of its shiny chrome-looking plastic trim deliberately blackened with permanent magic marker, the one with black duct tape slapped over both the broken battery door and the red LED function/recording light —you can hear what happened to me that night. But neither you nor I nor anyone else can tell exactly *when* it happened.

Since at the time I had made surveillance log entries every quarter hour, the incident occurred between 20:35 and 20:50. Yeah, I know 20:50 isn't on a fifteen minute interval, but I had missed the 20:45 entry because of what went down.

When you play the tape, this is what you hear:

"Hissssssssssssssssssssssssssssssssssss.

BANG CLUNK GALUNK FFFFFT FFFT BUMPCLUNK! Hissssssssssssss ssssssssssssssssssssss."

Followed by the roar of an engine and the squeal of tires spinning furiously on the streets of West Asheville.

I remember what it had looked like. First the bright lights, like auto high beams, and then my vision blotted out instantly. I remember my heart hammering fiercely, and my mind firing all of its guns at once in response to the unknown white void spreading out in front of me.

Am I shot? Am I dead? What the hell happened????

The hell that had happened was this: some unknown perpetrator had hurled an opened can of white house paint at the van's front windshield, then jumped in a vehicle and hauled ass.

Later that night, the crowd around the nearby Shell station started buzzing when I drove up—with my head sticking out the window—in the paint-splattered Soccer Mom van.

"Check it out, dawg . . . HATE to see the motherfuckin' bird who took THAT shit!"

"Hey, dawg! You tryin' to be Earl Scheib? You pimpin' yo' ride at night? You ain't starting RIGHT! $99 dollars for Bird Turd WHITE?! You know what I'm saying? Ho! "

How did I end up doing this? What miserable karmic debt am I repaying with this whole P.I. gig, anyway?

With my favorite little song of self-pitying playing over and over inside my head—a song accompanied by a chorus of powerful sighs coming from the high-pressure sprayer in my hands—I spent forty-five minutes at the car wash trying to remove the gallon of white paint from the rental van's windshield, hood, roof, fenders, tires, side mirrors, passenger door, front grille. During that time, when I hadn't been actively cursing my luck, I had been pondering imponderables.

Why in God's name did Kenny tell his wife? And why did someone throw a can of paint on me to make a point? Why didn't they just shoot me or throw a cinder block through the windshield, like normal people do when they catch P.I.'s on surveillance?

Yet all the while, and in spite of what happened, I had still been tempted to gloat.

After all, it had not been *oil-based* paint.

Chapter Eleven

The Poor Hunting the Poor: Serving Civil Process

Many other bread-and-butter P.I. assignments besides domestic stuck in my throat, no matter how hungry I was. Like serving civil process. In these mountains, process serving —locating witnesses and defendants; delivering lawsuits, subpoenas, and notices of repossession (e.g., telling people to hand over their mobile home)—was dangerous and dissatisfying. Southern Appalachia is still populated by proud, moody, reactionary, heavily-armed people who have sought this region as a refuge from—well, the very legal entanglements I would be drawing them into once I handed them those papers. And if the subjects had been affable, reasonable defendants, I wouldn't have received the assignment in the first place.

Moreover, the majority of difficult process assignments in my area were on the Nobodies, rarely on the Somebodies. No matter how much ingenuity or plain dumb luck I mustered, I could never get stoked about outwitting folks who were at the end of their rope, there but for the grace of God go I: *"Aha! I've finally found you! You're served with a Summons and Complaint . . . and sorry about your $75,000 default on those hospital bills!"* I was constantly reminded of the lyrics from a Scottish ballad that lament:

> *When the poor hunt the poor*
> *Over mountain and moor*
> *The rich man can keep them in chains.*

On the surface, serving civil process seems like easy money. Even the legal boilerplate language found in the North Carolina Rules of Civil Procedure makes it sound simple:

Rule 4. Process.

* * * *

(h1)Summons - When process returned unexecuted. - If a proper officer returns a summons or other process unexecuted, the plaintiff or his agent or attorney may cause service to be made by anyone who is not less than 21 years of age, who is not a party to the action, and who is not related by blood or marriage to a party to the action or to a person upon whom service is to be made . . . .

Yet the legalese barely hints at the monstrous problems lying beneath the surface of serving legal papers:

j) Process - Manner of service to exercise personal jurisdiction. - In any action commenced in a court of this State having jurisdiction of the subject matter and grounds for personal jurisdiction as provided in G.S. 1-75.4, the manner of service of process within or without the State shall be as follows:

(1) Natural Person. - Except as provided in subsection
(2) below, upon a natural person by one of the following:

a. *By delivering a copy of the summons and of the complaint to him or by leaving copies thereof at the defendant's dwelling house or usual place of abode with some person of suitable age and discretion then residing therein* [emphasis mine]

There it is. You have to find their home and serve them, or find them someplace else and do it there, even though all you usually have to go on is a name.

Process servers are like pizza delivery boys from Hell: we bring you something you didn't order, don't want, can't enjoy, and more than likely can't afford—but in the end you will pay dearly for, anyway.

In urban areas, where defendants' homes and businesses are easily identified and located within a few miles of each other and not too far from police patrols, process serving can be a lucrative and straight-forward matter, like being a mailman or meter reader. In rural areas, however, you must drive over horrendous distances and even worse roads, navigating by inadequate or flat-out wrong information contained in the legal papers—just to locate and personally serve someone whom the sheriff's department could not locate or serve and who will more than likely *not* be at home during normal business hours of nine-to-five. And to top it off, western North Carolina has *hundreds* of remote RV and camper parks—some listed, some not—and there are *thousands* of rental homes and cabins scattered throughout the mountains.

Still unconvinced? Here are some numbers to think about.

I have successfully served over three hundred (+300) individuals in a span of sixteen (16) years. To date, I have failed only three (3) times: 1) the defendant moved out of state; 2) the defendant killed herself the day before I finally found the trailer she couldn't afford, anyway; 3) defendant's lawyer interfered; had federal marshals intercept and detain me outside of the federal courthouse in Asheville so his client could flee (high-dollar lawyers trump P.I.'s when it comes to finger-pointing).

I usually charged between $50-$75 per service, sometimes more for very remote locations or urgent service. Each service assignment included at least three *good* attempts at service, photographic documentation of the residence and/or of the individual accepting (or refusing) the papers, courtesy phone call (usually long distance) to client confirming effective service.

More than fifty (50) percent of any given year's process service assignments arrived during three (3) months of the year—the winter holiday months of November, December and January.

Seventy (70) percent of adult rural North Carolinians were *not* at home between the hours of 8 AM and 6 PM. The thirty (30) percent that *were* home were usually a) sleeping because they worked 3rd shift; b) unemployed and desperate; or c) disabled by illness, injuries, medical malpractice or recent substance abuse binges.

More than sixty (60) percent of my assignments required me to figure out the actual current home address of the subject. One hundred (100) percent of the time I failed to charge adequately for the additional time and legwork required to find that erroneous 60%.

Eighty (80) percent of my process service assignments demanded that I negotiate successfully with the subject's dog(s), who seemed to fall in three (3) categories: 1) tiny hateful pampered little moppets who held their owners in utter thrall and who attached themselves to my feet and legs yapping all the while, begging me to step on them and accidentally launch World War III; 2) pit bull, Rottweiler, German Shepherd mix or Chow breeds who menaced my crotch while their owners guaranteed the dogs to be friendly—*before* you handed them the papers; 3) hunting dogs that would give the subject of your service attempt at least a ten (10) minutes heads-up that someone was coming, which was more than enough time to flee if you were evading service of process.

Chapter Twelve

Welcome to Country Time:
A Civil Process Story

I got a call from a P.I. out of Charlotte. He wanted me to serve papers on a woman out in my area.

In terms of a professional courtesy, I found it very hard to turn down service of process referrals, but I placed them on a much lower level of priority. But this P.I. was a pretty good guy, so when I got the papers late Friday afternoon, I went to serve them the following Saturday morning. And that was the day I discovered Country Time.

I crossed the French Broad River at Alexander, and meandered along the convoluted back roads towards the low-lying Turkey Creek/Sandymush area located in the northwest corner of Buncombe County. Like many farming communities that huddled against the walls of more impassable mountainous areas, this area was strangled by serpentine roads that hugged the rolling hills and crawled parallel to flood-prone creeks and bulged out of the way of the steeper inclines and even doubled back on themselves—anything to help the farmers have better access to markets. Of course, the local farmers knew the way and were not daunted by such commonplace puzzles as roads that suddenly go by another name without intersections or bridges or any damn explanation at all; the small white rectangular road signs that pointed the wrong way, if they existed at all; road signs that were missing, removed accidentally by livestock trailers and snow plows, or removed deliberately by drunken vandals and just contrary folk.

It was the damp cold of March, when crusty patches of undead snow clung to the north-facing pockets of trees and hillsides, and the chilling fog seemed to both squat down from the sky and push up from the land, smothering you all over. The medieval fear of "miasmas" came to mind—those noxious vapors once blamed for taking down entire villages. This was the weather that put lead in your bones, gravel in your lungs, coal in your soul. It was the month the old and the sick and the lonely die. Old timers will tell you that cattle, old folks and babies will die in September and March if they have anything wrong with them at all. You'll have to take their word on the cattle, but you can see for yourself about the people by walking around in the mountain cemeteries. Read the gravestones. Note especially the number of mossy markers with the little lambs etched on top—they're for the young'uns. Get permission first before you do this, though, because in North Carolina, you can still pretty much bury your own anywhere on a declared cemetery easement located upon private land—and that's as private as private land comes. You haven't felt the white-hot heat of a mountaineer's tetchi- ness until you've trespassed upon where Papaw John or Little Lucy Jean lie buried.

Preoccupied with such morbid thoughts, I almost drove right by the small bronze marker on the side of the road that indicated the address I was looking for: Country Time Village. A narrow blacktop drive led upward and disappeared into the fog-shrouded hills.

I backed up and pulled into the driveway and stopped. I got out and locked my truck's wheels in 4-wheel drive, in case there was ice or slush coating the way. I also looked over the papers I was serving while deciding what kind of ploy, if any, might be required to serve them. I had no idea what lay beyond the immediately visible fifty feet of driveway. I could not see any structures or other indications of what kind of residents lived at this mysterious development. There was a lettered sub-address appended to the numerical street address, suggesting maybe mobile homes, apartments, duplex units, rather than single residences comprising a sub- division. I decided that I had best put the papers inside my leather jacket and keep them out of sight until I got a better sense of what degree of subtlety was warranted.

My truck was a dark lonely blunt thing enveloped by a gelid curtain. The bare hills were just a penumbral presence beyond the nubs of white light pushing out from the headlights. The track narrowed to just the width of my tires. Like all such passages in heavy fog, it seemed to last much too long.

I saw little brown houses. Houses with dim yellow lights over their porches and doors. Several, maybe a dozen or so. They stretched along the inner rim and then circled around on top of the large bowl-shaped hillside that was pasture along the top, then dropped away below into an oblivion of dense forest, fallen gray tree bones and rotting leaves. I slowed to a crawl and turned off my headlights in order to—oddly enough—see more clearly. The houses seemed to emerge one by one, each accompanied by an ominous thrum of uncertainty. There were only a few cars clustered among the cabins. I rolled down the windows in order to sniff and hear the place. I smelled nothing. I heard nothing. There was no wind, and the cold wet air drove scent to the ground where it stayed.

As I approached the first house, I saw the unit number, and realized I had three more to go. I also realized that the houses were larger than they first appeared. They were almost like regular ranch houses. As I motored at a crawl past the first house, I observed no sign of life inside other than lighting.

I approached the second house, only a dozen yards past the first. A pale figure flitted into view from around the building and crossed the drive right in front of me. It turned out to be a large woman anywhere from fifty to seventy years of age, dressed only in a filmy white nightgown, her fleshy yellow-white arms hugged tight around herself, forming a "v" across her chest. As the woman floated by in the fog, I could see her fingers tapping rhythmically on her shoulders, tapping out a code or tune upon her bloated upper body that bent back and forth as she walked. She was also muttering to herself.

I swallowed hard and waited for her to clear the drive by several feet before creeping past her. As I passed by, I gave her the common rural salute of lifting one forefinger off the steering wheel and nodding my head. Through the open window came a husky, barking, seal-like voice, pronouncing one word over and over:

"Today . . . today . . . today . . . today . . . today . . . today. . . ."

I stared at her via the driver's side mirror as I drove away. Behind me a resigned, sour-sounding cry emerged from one of the cabins: "Shar-LEEN . . . git inside here before you freeze to death." Then the bang of a door shutting. The muttering woman stalked on, heedless.

The cold from the open windows pebbled my skin and lifted the hair from the back of my neck, so I rolled the windows up . . . only to realize that I was also sweating.

I arrived at the correctly numbered cabin. I smelled eggs and bacon. Heard voices and noises—*bird* noises—coming from inside. I saw lights glowing through the drawn curtains. A TV was on. Judging by the colored light flickering madly in the corner of one room and by the cacophony of voices, sound effects and musical flourishes, cartoons were showing. I noted there was one compact truck in the small parking lot. The truck bore an out-of-state license plate. I got out of my truck, walked warily towards the door, and knocked.

A drumbeat of feet, the whole cabin rattled, and then the door flew open.

My first thought was that I was being assaulted by enormous birds.

A stream of odd cooing and cackling and throaty chuckles hit me, followed by the soft percussion of limbs flapping all over me, patting my head, stroking my shoulders, then clutching at my arms with an alarming tenacity.

My welcoming committee continued to grin and flap and poke and claw at me. Sleep gummed the corners of their eyes; they smelled faintly of piss and baby powder. One of them wore the remnants of egg yolk around his tight grin; the other kept nodding savagely with some unknowable inner certainty as he patted

71

me down.

A gruff voice commanded from an unseen room: "Hey, now. . . Billy, Tee-Dee, leave'm be. Come on back and finish your breakfast."

The two greeters turned around and walked uncertainly towards the sound of the voice, occasionally stopping jerkily to look back at me, bashful smiles stretched across their faces. I looked across the room and saw, sitting in a wheelchair, positioned directly in front of the TV . . . well, I'm not exactly sure what I saw. The large head was covered with sparse, downy-looking hair; it lolled to the left and rear of the narrow shoulders; the eyes looked like busted grapes, sightless, wavering; the thin arms were drawn up tight at the elbows and the hands half-clenched in fists. The posture was that of a child waiting for someone to help put on winter mittens.

The wheelchair was parked next to a sagging sofa on which a solitary figure sat. The figure was hunched towards the TV in what appeared to be a state of rapt attention—so rapt, in fact, that I did not see him blink, nor did I see the rise and fall of his chest or back with the effort of breathing. He looked to be in his sixties; he had a rugged face and work-swollen hands that he held clenched together, fingers intertwined and propping up his chin. He wore a T-shirt with a packet of cigs in the chest pocket; blue jeans, and white socks which he rubbed together in tight little circles, the only part of him that moved. A large white scar ran down the middle of the sun-seared skin on the back of his neck.

I did not see or hear any women in this room. And I was there to serve papers on one.

A man appeared from around the corner of the kitchen, walking slowly, dressed in a fraying, rust-colored bathrobe, and a melon-colored T-shirt. He looked to be in his late thirties, with a stocky build and shoulder-length disheveled blonde hair. A cigarette hung from his cracking lips. His eyes bulged slightly, heavy-lidded, with purplish smears under the eyes. He took a deep drag and, looking thoughtfully at the cigarette for a second, proceeded to extinguish it in the crush of a hard-used hand.

"You doin' all right?"

"Doing pretty good . . . your breakfast smells like it's doing even better, though."

I told him straight out who I was and who I was looking for. He told me that the woman still worked up there at the rest home, but that the management switched things around, and he thought she now lived in one of the units up the road a ways. He asked me if she was in any trouble, and I told him not that I could tell. I allowed that this matter appeared to be a domestic concern, and that's about all there was to it. As he was talking, the heads of the welcoming committee peered around the corner, eyes goggling, frozen in their audacity. The blonde man followed the drift of my focus. He turned around and caught them in the act.

"I tole you to knock that shit off and eat your damn breakfast!"

The welcoming committee disappeared in an eyeblink.

He shook his head and pushed his unruly locks away from his face before he plunged his heavy fists into the pockets of his robe in a gesture of simmering agitation. He shook the pockets nervously, and I could hear a soft rattling sound inside the pockets. He stepped past me and looked out the window expectantly for a second, pulled one hand out of the robe pocket: a vial of prescription medicine. He frowned at the pills, looking mildly pissed off. He puffed his cheeks and blew across his lips in a dismissive gesture, gave a few hacking coughs and pocketed the pills again. He cut his eyes at me and uttered a low grumble: "I swear. . . retards will drive you up a wall, sometimes. I love 'em like family, but . . . *Jesus.*"

* * * * * *

Mountain people are extremely sensitive to criticism of any kind. Much of this sensitivity appears to be a consequence of being unfairly targeted for ridicule by city folks, and one area of their thin skin poked raw over time is that concerning their treatment of special needs individuals.

Only two generations ago, it was commonplace for families to keep around the home the ones who were deemed quare, fitified, lamed, or took spells. Solving a family's problem by turning them over to well-meaning neighbors just wasn't done, and giving them up to foreigners in the social services was unthinkable. The mountain regions were generally too poor to offer local care facilities, and even if kinfolk had the money, they wouldn't think of sending their quare or their old folks away because it would be like sending them to a sorrowful death: they would surely pine away and die once they were removed from the bosom of the mountains and their families. Also, given the isolation and privation of some mountainous regions, they kept these folks around for the same practical reasons they kept broken refrigerators, derelict cars, and old Mason jars: they weren't bad company; they could prove useful in a pinch; and there was no guarantee that a better replacement would be coming along directly.

Even today, some communities are quite protective about the quare ones, often finding in them special powers and talents. Local lore is rich in tales of their homegrown idiot savants; hilarious pinheads; babbling oracles; gifted musicians and whistlers; uncanny mimics who could lure wild game or mislead revenue agents away from bootlegger stills.

To be sure, it was always a highlight of my day to knock on the door of an isolated cabin surrounded by dozens of motor vehicles and find that all the folks were at work—except for the one they left at home to look after things. I never knew how it would go. The One They Left Behind could be a treasure-trove of information delivered gratefully and completely devoid of guile. Or could just be an enormous imbecile who filled the doorway with his vast bulk, hunching down to stare at me open-mouthed, eyes shining with dull delight at the new play toy that Providence had delivered to his door, greeting me with a gleeful roar: "HAR YOO DOO-WHEN? HUH? HAR YOO DOO-WHEN? AH'M DUKE! AH'M DUKE! YOO WAN' RASSLE ME?!"

But times change. Mountain people had become more exposed to the wealthier, consumer-oriented world of appearances that had typified to them the world of the flatlanders, they grew uncomfortable with the pointed questions about their quare ones and chafed under the derision that supposed their beloved mountains were inundated by milky-eyed, weak-chinned, banjo-playing defectives. Textile mills, industrial fabrication, and construction work took able-bodied men and women away from their farms for ten to twelve hours a day—these folks barely had time to take care of themselves and their healthy children. Southerners have proudly provided the backbone to our country's fighting forces, and so even more of the best and brightest were gone much of the time. Moreover, the ranks of those with special needs would who would require life care as the result of car accidents, industrial-related injuries, birth defects, chronic wasting diseases and drug abuse—would swell enormously.

Mountain people suddenly had a desperate need for care facilities they would have shunned only a generation or two ago. Privately-owned and operated adult "family care" assisted living centers answered that need, with facilities springing up throughout the WNC region in the most unlikely places, like daffodils.

But this scenario was not always as cheerful or as hopeful as the arrival of spring flowers. Without proper supervision, management, and regulatory oversight, "Adult Care Homes," "Rest Homes," "Family Care Homes," or "Assisted Living Centers" could become toxic dumping grounds for profoundly troubled individuals: convicted and paroled sex offenders who have been adjudicated as mental incompetents with no place else to go; drug addicts with mental illnesses ranging from attachment disorder to schizophrenia; elderly residents suffering from dementia and a host of life-threatening chronic illnesses like lupus, diabetes, cardiac or pulmonary congestion.

Poorly trained and overworked staff, limited budgets for governmental oversight, sporadic compliance reviews, a mountain heritage of "tough love" and "don't air your dirty laundry"—all of these factors promised trouble somewhere down the line. Isolated facilities like Country Time seemed like the fulfillment of that dark promise.

On the March day I arrived at Country Time, I had to visit three of the housing units in order to serve civil process. What I saw in each unit made me feel as though I were witnessing a time bomb of negligence ticking away unheard and unseen in the mountain mists. I told the Charlotte P.I. who hired me for the service of process about my experience: "Don't send me back out there again, man

. . . it's scary and it's a negligent care claim waiting to happen."

My misgivings would later prove to be well-founded, although I would learn that the problems there at Country Time had not gone entirely unnoticed. Later that same month, Buncombe County Department of Social Services would ask the NC Department of Health and Human Services - Division of Facility Services to close Country Time. DSS had cited the facility eighty-one times in seven years for violations ranging from improper supervision to failure to properly control and administer medications.

Country Time group homes did not close, however. In July of that year, a 57-year-old resident would collapse from heart failure after a 4th of July celebration there. DSS would report: "It was evident through interviews that residents and staff were aware of his deteriorating medical condition . . . but made no effort to contact his primary physician for follow-up or to return him to the emergency room."

Country Time underwent a name change and new management shortly after this death occurred in July 2003. Per DSS, the residents' care was reported to have improved as the result of the management change. However, a little more than a year later, a complaint had been filed against the new management in connection with the death of a 43-year old woman. The complaint alleged that the decedent did not receive adequate and timely follow-up care before her death on the morning of October 18, 2004. According to the new administrator, who was quoted in an *Asheville Citizen-Times* 10/25/2004 article, the resident did not die as a result of improper care: "She was a very sick woman," the administrator advised. "She was on dialysis and a diabetic. I think at one point she started refusing to eat."

Refusing to eat.

"I tole you to knock that shit off and eat your damn breakfast!"

I think about the two peculiar individuals who welcomed me to Country Time—the so-called "retards" who had aggravated the resident aide.

Officially, there were no mentally-retarded individuals living in that unit.

Chapter Thirteen

The Meeting

I t was 07:00 hours on a cool damp Saturday morning in April. I was sitting in the breakfast room of a chain hotel located just off I-40 in Greensboro. Except for the occasional metallic clank of food utensils and the morning mutter of the hotel staff preparing the self-serve hot meals, it was quiet. The roar of the interstate was absent now. At 09:00, a roar of another kind would erupt and ring in my ears for days once the meeting of NCAPI—the North Carolina Association of Private Investigators—commenced.

I declined the breakfast fare that steamed away in the stainless steel trays: blackened sausage patties, waxen scrambled eggs, greasy biscuits the size and consistency of hockey pucks, lukewarm and lumpy grits. I was not inclined to hit the miniature cold cereal boxes, nor optimistic enough for the so-called "fresh fruit" platters. I was eating a homemade fruit turnover and drinking green tea smuggled in via a small thermos wrapped inside a *USA Today*. I accepted some of the coffee, out of consideration for the breakfast room hostess. When she was not looking, I splashed some of this potent brew on a napkin and used it to clean my dress shoes that bore, despite all of my best efforts to the contrary, the signs of someone who literally just got off the farm.

As far as I could tell, I was the first P.I. at breakfast. Soon though, Monty, NCAPI's immediate past president who was also an early riser, joined me. We talked softly, mindful of who we were and what we did for a living and how early it was. Most of the NCAPI male officers and a loyal cadre of about a half-dozen male members showed up en masse around 08:30, speaking haltingly and exchanging painful grins as they recollected the money blown and liquor lost during the past night's debauchery at the strip club.

Other members trickled in around then, too. Some came to the breakfast bar in high spirits, wanting to socialize before the meeting started. Others came in stiff and slow, dragging the weight of last night's surveillance detail, their bleary eyes searching for glazed donuts and battery acid-strength coffee.

The meeting proper would take place in a small hotel conference room. But before that conference room filled with chirping pagers, tweedling cell phones, overpowering colognes, and the grunts and growls of contentious men and women too busy to explain and too distrustful of explanations to begin with—there was just the two of us there in the serene and frigid buffet room.

We enjoyed each other's company, yet we were an unlikely pair. He was a balding bear of a man in his early fifties; a tough, direct, plainspoken 11-year veteran of the Charlotte PD who rode Harleys and still swung his powerful arms in an exaggerated arc to clear the heavily-laden police duty belt he no longer wore. I was a sinewy, pony-tailed, feral-looking man in his early forties who could never quite mask his discomfort with enclosed spaces and fluorescent lighting.

We probably had more in common than we ever admitted to each other. We both realized that being a P.I. was a business first, a calling for those with an innately skeptical outlook on life second. We approached P.I. work not as a fantasy come true but as a highly-skilled trade. Just another difficult and strange way to make a living.

Four times a year NCAPI held their meetings, but it seemed that only once or twice a year did Monty and I get to have these early morning talks in which our guards were down. There was time enough to speak face to face without deadlines or other imperatives, time enough to talk without keeping score. I cherished those conversations all the more because as soon as breakfast was over and we wandered into a room filled with investigators, this friendly banter and free exchange of ideas disappeared. Our relationship became constrained, wary, and at times even adversarial.

We couldn't help it, though. Something ugly happened when P.I.'s grouped.

Blame it on the bad coffee, the lack of sleep, the workload (whether too much or too little). Blame domestic cases or ex-spouses or Satan or overindulgence in spicy wings and strong drinks the night before. All theories of causation were equally valid but still insufficient to explain the mysterious chemical reaction that occurred, turning even the most decent and thoughtful and diplomatic among us into hair-triggered rancorous jerks whenever three or more of us gathered to discuss our profession.

I admit that I have divided loyalties towards my task of portraying P.I. culture. I am torn between committing stoic self-censure and obscenity-riddled rants; between protecting my fellow P.I.'s and whaling away at them mercilessly like a domestic squabble gone bad. I hope that I can convey the complicated relationship that exists among P.I.'s without bouncing between the walls of extremes, or resorting to stereotypes or armchair psychoanalysis.

To be sure, trying to describe exactly why P.I.'s didn't get along is like trying to pick up one fishhook out of a pile of hundreds. But I would hazard to suggest that in general, we antagonized with our best intentions and harmonized with our worst, just like any other dysfunctional group.

For a given year, NCAPI's membership ran between 120 –150 members out of more than 1000 licensed P.I.'s across the state. Out of this pool of licensees, only about a third were active, full-time investigators. For a given NCAPI meeting, if thirty investigators who were not also NCAPI officers (eight officers) showed up, it was considered a full house.

The explanations behind the general P.I. apathy towards the NCAPI—as well as those for why NCAPI itself was so polarized and ineffectual—were many, and each one could be debated endlessly. What was undeniable, though, was the consequence to the profession's lack of cohesiveness: we had no effective, unified voice with which we might have protected and improved our livelihoods.

We were a fiercely independent bunch. We were pitted against each other in a profession that suffered what must have been one of the highest rates of attrition for any legitimate information-driven business. Excellent service did not guarantee client loyalty, nor did it automatically deliver a steady income. Even those P.I.'s who had police and military pensions to eat from—those who slashed their fees to the bone, trying to survive by swiping business from some other P.I.— mostly failed to make it on their own. They may have been fortunate enough to milk a part-time security guard job, or borrow from a hard-working spouse, or literally moonlight enough subcontract domestic cases peeping on the cheaters and beaters to stay afloat for awhile. But it took only one bad mistake, one unhappy client who was highly litigious or very slow paying or both—to make the bubbles of their gumshoe dreams go *POP!* in the night. Or in bankruptcy court. Or sometimes in divorce court, wherein the P.I.'s spouse would demand everything short of blood sacrifice as compensation for all those long erratic hours spent disregarding birthdays, anniversaries, holidays, vacation plans, illnesses.

If you had slipped into that conference room before the meeting began, you would have been surprised. First you would have seen an assembly of mostly overweight, out-of-shape men and women between the ages of thirty to fifty-five, all neatly dressed in the typical suburban weekend uniforms of double-knit shirts and jeans or khaki slacks. Taking a longer look, you would have noticed a few young men in there with military-type haircuts and strapping builds; one man with a pony-tail who seemed to be scanning the room for escape hatches; and maybe one or two overdressed young women with factory tans and hair that was, as beauticians describe it, "fried, dyed, and laid by the side." There would be an almost 5:1 ratio of men to women.

Before the meeting started, all of the folks inside the conference room would be sitting there peacefully enough. They would be quietly arranging their notepads, briefcases, cell phones and PDA's, settling into the cold plastic and chrome chairs, sipping from coffee mugs. They would peer at each other with mildly expectant looks aimed through eyeglasses that perched lightly on their own noses, and sometimes nod or wink at each other in silent familiarity. They would resemble at a distance the typical participants of any adult education class or civic club meeting you would find anywhere in the country.

Don't you believe it.

There were some extremely dangerous people in that room. And I don't mean just the ones who were armed.

The majority of the folks in there spent years in the military and/or in law enforcement, where they developed a formidable acuity for detecting weakness of any kind. That faculty, coupled with the scorpion's sense of fair play they acquired along the way, gave them the competitive edge they needed. They were capable of dealing with perps, creeps, and lying dirtbags on a daily basis, and still had strength enough left over to fight their real enemies: the *hundreds* of newly-licensed P.I.'s that arrived in NC every year.

Service in the military and/or in law enforcement was the preferred and most prevalent background for P.I.'s in North Carolina, particularly for those intent upon working in fields of executive protection ("EP" for short) and criminal defense work. But such backgrounds did not guarantee reliability or even competence in other investigative areas.

Moreover, when ex-LEO backgrounds created the prevailing mindset within a professional association, these backgrounds often hindered as much as helped. From their experience as either victims or perpetrators of bureaucratic infighting, many of these service veterans had become adept at "checking 6 (as in 6 o'clock, the position to your rear)" or CYA (Covering Your Ass). They were masters in the dark arts of the stonewall response, the good cop/bad cop interrogation, the confidential leak, the blackball campaign, the calculated innuendo, the vicious prank, the long-range smear.

These tactics had their usefulness. However, their frequent deployment against fellow P.I.'s in response to slights real or imagined—in response to virtually anything they perceived as threatening to their *status quo*—helped create a toxic environment of intimidation and divisiveness in the profession, a climate in which true innovation and improvement could not thrive. Even worse, too many of them came to the meeting carrying the weight of the worst Southern legacies: race-baiting, bare-knuckled politicking, union busting, and a thoroughly Calvinist conviction of the total depravity of everyone but themselves.

As for the P.I.'s who did not come to the profession by way of the military or law enforcement, by and large they were like the gifted mutants portrayed in the *X-Men* films. They brought to the meeting an amazing array of forensic capabilities, analytical skills, photographic memories, computational wizardry, innate lie detecting, uncanny mimicry, irresistible powers of verbal persuasion. No job but this one seemed to accommodate their peculiar aptitudes, and they were all too aware of their precarious Misfit Toy status. Thus they were determined to keep their P.I. gig at any cost.

Ironically, the cost could include betraying all P.I.'s by selling sensitive trade secrets and insider knowledge to the general public.

While my fellow P.I.'s from the military or law enforcement might have misplaced personal loyalties at times, they at least *had* them. They would stand by their select comrades and stick to their time-honored code of silence regardless of the professional consequences. My so-called "civilian" colleagues, on the other hand, too often lacked any sense of professional loyalty. Many were blown into the profession during the '90s, riding the high-tech winds of change like a locust swarm. And they duly acted the part of utterly self-regarding creatures focused only upon serving the demands of their own feeding frenzy. They were usually far too eager to allow the marketplace to decide any and all ethical considerations. And since they were the ones who usually did not have service pensions, they would be the first to go if or when the marketplace forced them out of business.

We were not all bad people. That sounds so lame to say, but it's good for me to reiterate it, anyway, like a meditation mantra.

We were not all bad people. P.I.'s did not act any differently than other highly-competitive service industry professionals. What we wanted, we wanted very very badly. And we often behaved very badly as a consequence.

We wanted magic words, invisibility cloaks, X-ray vision, mind-reading capability, boundless energy—the usual stocking-stuffers that white-collar professionals craved—to help us obtain the information we sought. We wanted just compensation for the interminable hours we kept. We wanted less to do and more time in which to do it. We wanted disability benefits for being just who we were, since once you were a P.I. you could not hold any other type of employment without going batshit from boredom. We wanted respect for our knowledge of how the world *really* worked—no, we wanted *vindication* for that knowledge.

We are what we are, something that both God and Popeye once said.

We were hardwired to chase the unknown, like so many sled-dogs or scent hounds.

We were designed to be human lockpicks destined by chance or by choice to be thrust roughly and repeatedly into the complicated mechanisms of human nature, staying whole for as long as we could while unlocking secrets, until we broke apart inside some dark closure that was beyond our skill and reckoning and we were finally discarded.

I ran across many brilliant, compassionate, trustworthy P.I.'s out there, in North Carolina and throughout the South, from all different backgrounds. The majority of accomplished P.I.'s were dedicated to serving their clients and assisting other P.I.'s with their cases. They were content to stay out of partisan politics and well below the radar of media hype or legal scrutiny or both. Even the most growly, grizzled old veterans were at heart decent men and women who didn't suffer fools and challenges to their authority. When I considered their experiences, I could not blame them.

There was a small but extremely influential minority who were attracted to the profession for the darkest reasons. It was this minority that earned most of the public notoriety and most of my spleen. These were damaged and damaging creatures who felt that they had been robbed of the necessary breaks to profit from their malevolence to the extent that, say, politicians had. They were bullies, shakedown artists, legal blackmailers who preyed upon those credulous or unfortunate enough to have crossed their path. They swelled with self-righteousness whenever their hasty judgments and poor research skills were questioned—which was daily—and they coalesced into the morass of cronyism known as the Good Ole Boy system to protect their individual incompetence.

If you were a P.I. and you crossed the Good Ole Boys once, maybe you'd be warned by a couple of sophisticated crank calls, or maybe your FAX machine would be jammed for days. Cross them again and you'd wonder just who made that phone call that got you burned on that big surveillance detail you had been planning for weeks. Or why your power or gas was cut off by "mistake." Maybe you'd start getting pornographic materials in the mail. Or you'd find yourself kicked off a P.I. online chat group—but not before your computer had been hacked or fake email messages sent all over the Internet under your forged signature line.

Well, we were all in that conference room together. The Good Ole Boys. The White Knights. The cynics. The greedy. The lazy. The workaholics. The posers. The fundamentalist Christians. The hypocrites. The ex-realtors, ex-paralegals, ex-accountants, ex-cops, ex-soldiers, ex-car salesmen, ex-plumbers, ex-electricians, ex-teachers, ex-Yankees. It was a free-for-all. The Piedmont against the Western mountains, Raleigh against Charlotte, the city against the country, age against youth, men against women, civilians against military, criminal work against civil, 9mm pistols against .45's, digital against analog, Chevy against Ford.

The high-minded purposes to which our professional association was dedicated, and for which we were gathered—seemed doomed from the start. The minute we closed that conference room door, we would fracture into puzzle pieces so intricately shaped that even the most dedicated investigators could not put us together.

To even further complicate such gatherings, our association meetings took place the day after the seasonal Private Protective Service Board (PPSB) meetings. Logistics dictated this, but holding our NCAPI meetings after these PPSB sessions was like trying to plan a vacation after receiving a pink slip from work and a notice of an IRS audit all on the same day.

The PPSB was the regulatory board working under the aegis of the NC Department of Justice to govern the licensure and conduct of private investigators, burglar alarm and premise surveillance installers, electronic counter-surveillance technicians, armed and unarmed security guards, polygraph operators, guard dog trainers and handlers. PPSB investigated public complaints against P.I.'s and P.I. complaints against unlicensed activity. They suspended licenses, denied applications, and fined individuals for investigative misconduct. They searched the backgrounds and credit-worthiness of applicants and determined who would be licensed or not. Since credit problems plagued virtually all P.I.'s caught in the high-overhead, feast-or-famine nature of their profession, this particular licensure requirement gnawed away at them like a rat on a corncob. PPSB also decided how much it would cost a P.I. to obtain or renew their licensure, and how much liability insurance and continuing education they would require.

Most full-time P.I.'s seemed to regard the PPSB with fear and loathing, steering as wide a berth around it as possible. P.I.'s who joined NCAPI, however, soon learned to work themselves into an unsightly froth over every decision made or not made by PPSB, and to stay frothy throughout the NCAPI meeting that ensued. In the past, the PPSB's most persistent critics were those P.I.'s who were actually scheming to get themselves elected to the PPSB board. They dreamed of achieving a bureaucrat's status, with which they could actively demoralize and loot the troops, and not merely passively bitch and moan about such atrocities during NCAPI meetings.

Although NCAPI was created in 1987 as a voluntary professional association purportedly dedicated to boosting the effectiveness and the morale of private investigators, the meetings themselves seemed to achieve the exact opposite. Debate was encouraged but all questions were suspect. Open dissent was admonished and the dissenters ostracized or targeted for whispering campaigns. Several NCAPI meetings ended just short of an outright brawl. The growing presence of female investigators seemed to offer little in the way of mitigating those testosterone-charged clashes. On the contrary, women seemed to exacerbate the pissing contests, either because the men assumed that the women were the perfect impressionable audience for those contests, or because the women themselves had learned to act in a manner that was just as contentious, opinionated, and short-sighted as their male counterparts.

Robert's Rules of Order limited the open combat to sniping and setting booby traps. But perversely enough, this thin veneer of civility only perpetuated the warfare because the hostilities were often cloaked in procedural maneuvers. Thus, NCAPI appeared to reach a new resolution every meeting—a resolution to keep squabbling ineffectually over the same issues . . . forever. And just when consensus might have been reached on one issue, the issue would somehow morph into another seemingly implacable foe, like the cyborgs in the *Terminator* films.

For example, there was the issue of badges.

At one time, our P.I. credentials bore a glued-on passport-sized photo along with the NC state seal and the NC PPSB logo. They looked like the fake ID's we used in high school back in the '70s. Then our credentials were redesigned with a digitized copy of our photo and a brightly-colored NC State Seal and NC PPSB logo. They might have been convincing and effective enough for identification purposes if they hadn't resembled something a bored 5-year-old had produced with an Etch-A-Sketch and a handful of crayons.

Metallic badges appeared authoritative and commanded more respect, and many P.I.'s yearned to experience both of these things. At the time, however, North Carolina General Statute Chapter 74-C, which governs the actions of PPSB and all that falls within their domain, expressly forbade wearing, carrying, or even accepting "any badge or shield purporting to indicate that the person is a private detective or private investigator while licensed under the provisions of this Chapter as a private investigator." § 74C-12, Subsection A, paragraph (12)

The fear of P.I.'s blurring the line between themselves and sworn law enforcement officers—of someone flashing the badge and intimidating folks into divulging information—was deeply-rooted in all P.I.'s who were ex-LEO's and who were therefore all too familiar with the ways a badge could be abused. Yet some ex-LEOS and many other P.I.'s from non-law enforcement backgrounds felt that a P.I. badge neither compelled nor condoned misconduct any more than a police badge did. It was the professionalism and integrity of the individual wearing the badge that were the real issues, they said. To instill a sense of the former and to symbolize the importance of the latter, they felt that badges were necessary. They also argued that badges kept people from interfering with surveillance stakeouts and field interviews in rough neighborhoods.

There was never any pretense of a civil debate on this issue. All arguments either for or against badges were predicated upon attacking the opponent's personal credibility.

Me? I didn't need no stinkin' badge. I would have liked an identification card that didn't look like I bought it at Toys 'R' Us, though.

But the issue of badges was not just about the issue of badges.

It was also the issue of whether executive protection operators required distinct and much more rigorous licensure requirements than P.I.'s who merely had an armed carry endorsement to their licenses.

And the issues of badges and EP licensure bled over into the issue of why P.I.'s who possessed CCW permits (concealed weapons permits) and who did not carry weapons for hire but only for their personal protection—had to maintain the costly and burdensome armed carry endorsement as well as the correlative armed carry liability insurance.

And when the members had harangued and blustered and browbeaten the breath out of each other on these matters, the issues of increased continuing education requirements or firearms instructor re-certification would rear their ugly heads and galvanize them back to fractious life again.

In short, at the heart of all contentious P.I. issues lay the question of *credibility*.

Who may or may not be licensed, or hired as associates or subcontractors, or carry weapons while on duty, or sweep premises for eavesdropping devices, or provide EP services? These questions of credibility continued to be addressed in the bold-typed, black and white imperatives of *skills, training, experiences.*

But in the private investigator profession—in the security industry itself—there was nothing even *close* to a general agreement on how to measure the effectiveness or even the relevancy of *skills, experiences, training* in a world that seemed to change more rapidly each year. Given the staggering range of investigative expertise required to accommodate our clients—who occupied an even broader range of social, political, and geographical peculiarities—what were the uniform standards by which professional credibility was measured? Elite military training? Number of continuing education seminars? Number of clients? Number of employees? Number of years in the business? Yearly income? Personal credit score? Most expensive equipment? Least amount of stress? Lack of visible facial tics, sewer breath, by-pass operations, prescription med dependencies?

The question of *credibility* was ultimately a philosophical one. And it has been my experience that P.I.'s would rather tear off and eat their own ears before they would ever delve deeply into philosophical questions. And then only after tearing off and eating someone else's ears *first*.

Chapter Fourteen

War Stories

T hey say that as you get older, your memory grows tired and selectively replays only the good times.

If true, then this must be another natural law that doesn't apply to P.I.'s. Because from what I've seen, it seems that the longer you are a P.I., the more your memory fixates on the bad and loses track of the good.

When P.I.'s bothered to listen to each other—which was almost never—it was the negative and cautionary tales they would hear. The fuck-ups, the betrayals, the begrudgery, the missed opportunities—these formed the backbone of P.I. "war stories" which were, themselves, much more than token attempts at confessional conviviality. They were investigative techniques in their own right. If you wanted to jack up the cost of an assignment to a client, you'd tell a war story fraught with dire implications for a less costly effort. If you wanted to dissuade a particularly aggressive P.I. from infiltrating your turf and snake-charming your clients away, a shocking little vignette filled with catastrophes would make him look elsewhere. There was nothing original or even particularly clever about this approach, but it worked. That's why the Vikings named a hunk of ice "Greenland" and a island with natural hot tubs "Iceland." That's why ancient maps have the legend "Here be Dragons" blocking the easiest navigation routes.

But while I do seem to recall the bad more than the good over the years, I used my own precedents or war stories to scare myself, not others, into the appropriate state of mind or proper behavior essential to my survival as a P.I.

For example, think how instructive it was for me to recall that I once almost killed myself with a pair of "Billy Bob Teeth." You know, those costume dentures with the inflamed gums and big gaps between the two or three remaining rotten teeth? Stupidest thing I ever did, I swear. This is how it happened.

I had to discreetly eyeball a subject while he made a court appearance for a child custody hearing, then follow him wherever he went after that. No one knew where the subject was actually living. I had to find that out in order to watch him, and the courthouse appearance was my only good chance. But the courthouse in question was the Yancey County courthouse, where I was well-known and where I couldn't take the chance that one of the clerks or title searchers working there might unintentionally burn me by hollering their favorite friendly greeting of "HEY THERE! NOW WHO ARE YOU SPYIN' ON UP HERE?"

So I had the brilliant idea of wearing thick eyeglasses, an earring, and the least disgusting model of Billy Bob Teeth I could find. I dressed in an auto repairman's uniform (polyester pants and shirt with repair shop logo). I reasoned that if I didn't look like me—and somewhat repulsively so—I might be ignored.

Well, the get-up actually worked. I grunged my way into the courthouse, right past the sharp eyes of female court clerks and paralegals, none of whom gave me more than a quick glance. I sat in the courtroom and waited. About a half-hour into my wait for my subject's case to be called, I began to feel a strange heat spreading out underneath and around the dentures. I ignored the feeling at first, thinking it was just the overheated courthouse air giving me fits. About twenty minutes more and I realized my throat was on fire and I could barely swallow. Couple minutes more and my upper lip started tingling and swelling and feeling like it just came back from a two-hour workout at the dentist's office. *What's this?* I worried as I began to choke as quietly as I could without attracting attention in a crowded courtroom.

Finally my subject's case was called. When his lawyer finished talking to him, he stalked out of the courtroom. I stumbled after him, snorting and gasping, tears streaming down my face from suppressing my gag reflex. As my subject exited the courthouse, I staggered behind a privet hedge and radioed my backup.

"Woonit won, Woonit won, do woo copy?

"Roger Unit 2—go ahead. You sound funny, like you're talking through a voice scrambler."

I can't talk! I'm turning into Donald Duck!

"Woonit won—shubjecks OUT. Weepeet-shubjecks OUT. Adwize white mwale, bwown-checked long-shleeve shirt, shleeves wolled up; shtone-wassed jeans, gwold-colwed shpowat shwoos. Do woo have viz-oo-al?"

"Roger that, Unit 2 – I have visual. Quit talking like that."

But I couldn't quit talking like that. Because I was having an allergic reaction to the adhesive used to cement the Billy Bob teeth to my palate, and my mouth and throat were closing fast. A look at my reflection in the courthouse door glass told me I was beginning to resemble The Elephant Man. I was going to die as the

Elephant Man named Billy Bob. My backup followed our subject and learned where he lived, while I almost stopped breathing . . . .

Then there was the time I served some trailer repo papers on a mother of two who had been hiding for months. She had this bad-ass boyfriend who worked part-time for a mobile home service outfit, and part-time for the county jail whenever he went to liquoring up and beating her down. When her mortgage checks bounced, she would get her boyfriend to snatch her trailer and move it in the dead of night. The finance company went apeshit trying to figure out how and to where this trailer kept moving. Well, I found out what kind of car she was driving and where her kids were going to elementary school. I interviewed all the school bus drivers and discovered that the only time she showed herself to the daylight was when she dropped off or picked up her kids at the bus stop. So one afternoon I found her waiting at one of the bus stops, and I served her just as the bus pulled up. I called her name and she turned around slow. When she looked at me she kind of stiffened all over, like someone who just had an icy hand drop onto the back of their neck. Her kids ran up to her the second after I handed her the papers and explained what they were. Well, she threw the papers back at me and started hollering: "YOU CAN'T DO THIS . . . YOU'RE NOT AN OF-FICIAL PERSON. KIDS . . . YOU WITNESSED THIS, THIS IS ILLEGAL, YOU SAW WHAT I DID, I NEVER TOUCHED THOSE PAPERS!" Her kids started screaming at me, too, "YOU LEAVE OUR MOMMY ALONE!" Then they chased after me as I fairly jogged towards my truck parked about a block away. The whole time these kids were throwing rocks, crab apples, sticks, dogshit, whatever they could get their hands on and fling at me, yelling "CREEPY MAN! CREEPY MAN!" the whole way . . . .

Or how about when I was serving some papers out in Cullowhee and got pinned in the bed of my own pickup truck for forty minutes by a swift, swirling black cloud that turned out to be two dogs: a Bouvier des Flandres the size of a pony and his agent provocateur, a formerly friendly Labrador Retriever? The only way to get back into my truck was to feed the Bouvier the legal document I was supposed to be serving . . . .

And then there's the time I was perched in a tree during surveillance and wild turkeys landed in the branches above me and their gooey shit splattered down all over me. I had to tell my wife about that case, she was bound to find out about it, anyway, I mean, the smell alone. . . .

That reminds me . . . there was this woman down in Rutherfordton who wit-nessed horrific acts of abuse and neglect at a nursing home where she worked. She was frightened out of her skin about being a whistleblower witness, more freaked out than a cat caught in a car wash. But I had to keep her talking so the facts would come out of her in spite of herself, her recollections coughed up like just so many spitty hairballs.

You haven't lived unless you've been trapped for three hours inside of a shut-fast, kerosene-heated, nicotine-drenched mobile home with a nervous chain-smoker who has been both waiting for and dreading the arrival of someone like me, someone who finally "wants to hear my side of the story, " a story that, unfortunately, keeps changing every time she resumes telling it after being interrupted by the treadmill of events that make up the sum of her heroic yet profoundly chaotic existence: several collect phone calls from her teenage daughter in jail; trying to get her VCR to record a program for her oldest son, who wants to be a NAS-CAR mechanic, and then cursing the VCR and searching the whole trailer for the directions and then calling one of her kin to find out how to set the VCR, only to talk to the said older son who tells her he won't be coming home that night and so she just turns the volume of the TV up in anger and shouts over it, which plays hell with the tape-recording I am trying to make; having to pull one toddler away from a floor fan that blows the nose-crisping kerosene heat over the room in noxious waves, and then wiping puppy shit off another toddler, who isn't really hers but actually her sister's baby "and he's just a mess," and then rescuing a pair of struggling puppies who've become stuck fast in one of her youngest son's soccer cleats—"I love Chow pups —don't they look just like little baby bears?"; fixing an absent-minded sandwich for no one in particular, which will sit on the counter for an hour or so before she begs me to eat it and I will die a thousand deaths before finally ignoring the cigarette ash and other unknown debris smudged over the white bread and eat it, washing it down with a diet Pepsi that I couldn't drink again with a gun to my head; lighting two or three cigarettes at a time that she will leave on various countertops while sifting through a foot-thick stack of pay envelopes, utility bills, medical care invoices, copies of temporary restraining orders against a boyfriend, discount coupon books, etc., in order to find her notebook wherein she documented hundreds of instances of nursing home abuse; searching frantically for one of her kid's Thanksgiving Day cards, a dark-cray oned creation of a hand and thumb-outline "Tom Turkey" that supposedly bears a missing witness' phone number that is "so life and death important to me it's unreal" but she can't remember the phone number nor find the right thumb-turkey that has the phone number on it, which makes her cry and then run off to her bedroom to find what she calls her "crybaby pills," all the while begging me to "please believe me . . .I'm not crazy, honestly, I'm not, you got to believe me, all that stuff that happened is true, I swear to God, it's just been so long ago, and it's been so hard on me with these kids and all, and with knowing what I know about those sweet old ladies suffering like that, it just takes me time to think of anything or find anything in here . . . ."

There was this dyslexic and speech-impaired young man barely making it through his freshman year of college. He was handsome and a gifted artist, but so shy and sensitive that almost every new encounter forced his eyes to goggle and mist over, and his throat to emit strangled frog noises. He took up binge drink-ing to lubricate his jammed social skills, and this time-honored compensation mechanism worked well. Until one day he found himself trapped in a cubicle and paralyzed by the reptilian gaze of police detectives who wanted to know all about the frat party he had attended and what he knew about the 2nd degree rape and sodomy of a coed who was bigger, stronger, drunker and—at first—more willing than he had been.

For *him*—not for his family, not for the client's attorney, not even for the money—for *him* I struggled, working through the chaos that is inherent in all Young People Fucked Up at Parties crime scenes. Then the trial began, and all my hard work would be tested. My client looked small and vulnerable, clearly overwhelmed by his predicament and by his yellow paisley tie. His lawyer had coached him to appear calm and avoid panic seizures by writing things down on a yellow legal pad whenever he had questions or became nervous. The entire legal pad was filled with doodles and drawings of his alter ego, Snoopy, who suffered page after page of varying mortal dilemmas, all of which were depicted with vir-tuosity and depth of feeling. The last drawing portrayed a recumbent Snoopy with X's for eyes and a tombstone at his head. A ghostly thought balloon issued forth from the now lifeless beagle, and contained this scrawled judgment: "Im not gon mak it in this lif."

But my client was wrong! And the DA was wrong! And the victim was wrong! And Snoopy rejoiced, dancing on the cardboard backing of the legal pad with his characteristic blur of happy paws!

Because the jury foreman said "Not Guilty" to the rape and sodomy charges! And the legal pad filled with Snoopy's misadventures, and all the other legal pads filled with the attorneys' terse comments, legal motions and citations, jury selec-tion strategies, etc., were destroyed—including a note that my client's attorney stuffed into my pocket: "*Sit on that witness until trial is over.*"

That witness. . . the one who called me midway through the trial.

"Hey, I heard you were on campus interviewing people about that party where the girl got raped."

"Yeah, I was, but I don't think we'll need to talk to you now. The trial is un-derway, and we have a lot of witnesses already. No need in dragging you down here. Thanks for calling, though."

That witness . . . whom the detectives and university police had never inter-viewed and indeed whose very existence was still unknown to them . . . whom none of the other witnesses could recall . . . who left school shortly after the inci-dent, and therefore remained in the dark about the ongoing investigation . . . who talked to no one at the school about the incident, including the victim . . . and who corroborated the victim's account of every tortured word she uttered, every sordid, violent action that she suffered. *That* witness.

I even met a witch once. No, I'm not kidding, she was the real deal, or as real as I want to meet, given the circumstances. I was in Mitchell County in late July, up near Double Island, and I got hit by one of those late afternoon gully-washer rains—the kind that makes you think you've suddenly driven into a car wash. I crossed over the North Toe River at the Rose's Branch bridge, and the river was close to flood stage: all roiled, angry, scary-looking, surging wildly against the concrete bridge abutments, pushing logjams through the tumbling waves, whole trees plowing along on what looked like all the Chocolate Yoo-Hoo ever made in the world pouring through there. I should have turned back but I was trying to locate a trucker who had witnessed a fatal collision in the Pigeon River Gorge area of I-40 near the Harmon's Den exit. Seemed this fellow didn't live *anywhere* except in his Kenilworth truck. He just showed up when his dispatcher needed him. All I had to go on was the phone number of his aunt, who seemed to know how to get in touch with him. But the aunt never answered the phone the half-dozen or so times I called her, so I had to go on out there and see what was up. It's just that way with me. The more difficult it was to find someone or get a hold of them, the more stubborn I got about not turning loose until I did.

Anyway, I found the aunt's place after three or four drives past the location where the county property records suggested it would be. It turned out to be one of those old-timey houses with the rough poplar slab-siding so dark and moldy and swallowed up by vegetation you couldn't tell where the house started or the woods ended, and you sure couldn't believe anybody lived in there, let alone had electricity and a phone. By the time I pushed my way through the heavy down-pour and through the even heavier boxwood hedges and jewelweed thickets on my way to the front door, I was soaked. I was about to knock on the door and click—the door just opened up. I hate when that happens.

Well, there's this tiny old woman standing there. She came up to about my chest, maybe, in height and she had her gray hair pulled back in a tight bun on top of her head. She wore a dirty blue smock with yellow flowers on it and some kind of stretch pants or leggings. She had a pale angular face deeply lined and sharp-chinned; her thick gray brows sprouted black hairs here and there including a few on the bridge of her large reddened nose, which looked more like a curved beak except for the huge dark pores pitting the surface. Her face was definitely distinct but looked unfinished, as if someone whittled her out of basswood and stopped before smoothing her out. She didn't look up at me at first; she looked straight at my chest when she spoke: "I knew you were a-comin' today. Come in. You don't want to be out there in that rain, you'll likely fall down the bank and down the river you'll be, like a dead sycamore tree." She talked quietly but her voice was so clear and penetrating that it made my ears ring. She had that reedy twang of the area, saying "sicky-more" for sycamore. In the past I have heard people say they "knew" I was coming, even though I hadn't ever mentioned to anyone that I was looking to talk to them. But none of them had ever said it as matter-of-factly as she did, like our meeting had been predestined.

So I stepped through the doorway and entered her house. It was all dark and muggy inside. A single fluorescent bulb glowed eerily near the kitchen window, an old Knox cookstove smoked slightly, a sour wet wood smell joined the musky, tantalizing aroma left over from thousands of bacon and biscuit meals fixed over the years. Once inside, the woman turned her back on me and kept walking toward the gloomy kitchen and I followed, while at the same time looking at the faded wallpaper made from old newspapers and Christmas wrapping coated with shellac except for the Jesus portraits hanging upon the walls and upon the chalky kitchen cupboards. I walked into the kitchen just behind her until she stopped and turned around. Her heavy upper eyelids flipped up like a plastic doll's and Zzzt! she hit me with those eyes.

To this day I couldn't tell you if they were green, brown, blue, whatever. All I remember is the way those eyes gleamed. Her eyes had an unusual steely sheen to them, like the way the river shines on an early winter morning when the sky glides over the rippling water. And at the same time I noticed she had one of those little dogs that fits into a pocket—I couldn't tell what kind of dog it was because it was just a pair of dark eyes and tippy little ears, a tiny snout and a topknot of fur sticking out of a pocket.

I always get a kick out of those people who keep those "pocket poodles" or "tit terriers" or whatever you want to call them. But I swear I didn't see the damn thing in her smock pocket when she came to the door. So when she flipped her eyelids up and nailed me in place with her metallic stare and commenced speaking in her metallic voice—all I knew was that my skin started prickling and my legs became a numb blob beneath me and I was as scared of being in this smoky cave of a room with this little woman and her puppet dog as I had ever been in any other hairy situation I could remember.

So she spoke, saying "I knew you was a-comin' . . . because I have The Second Sight." And she proceeded to tell me how she didn't ask for this gift; that The Maker gave it to her just like he gave her lupus and "The Sugars," (what local folks call diabetes), and she said she didn't ask for them, either, but her "spells" come and go as they please and they bring along her visions, which come to her sudden-like, like the way "the moon comes sailin' through the clouds." Between her and the dog there were four eyes not blinking—she stared at me and the dog stared at me and her voice fell out of her mouth and jangled around the room like a bag of coins spilling onto the oak floor. The rain had been hammering on the tin roof in a steady roar, sounding like a truckload of gravel being dumped up there. But her voice cut clean through it. She told me she knew I was hunting for her nephew, and that I must be good at what I do because I sure didn't look like no private detective. Well, I never said anything about who I was or why I was there but she seemed to know, anyway. And I was thinking maybe the trucking company dispatcher told her, so that settled my nerves a bit.

She started to tell me about myself, saying that mostly I was a quiet man, patient and still like a heron, but I was too full of strong feelings and these feelings would get me to acting fretful like a setting hen. She said there was a man, a big man, a giant—"a John't"—who had the heart of a little boy, and he was watching over me, protecting me, and that he held a little bird that would land on me one day with a message of joy just for me. This would all happen if I'd just "get right with The Maker."

She reached up with one hand and began to rub her shoulder just above the pocket dog. At first I thought she was going to pet the dog, but she rubbed her shoulder slowly, methodically, moving her fist in a circular pattern over the shoulder, like someone mixing cake batter, with her gaze fixed straight ahead and that freaky dog still as a statue and both of them with the same eyes. She said she had the "arthur-itis" and on her bad days she couldn't do for herself as she ought, as she felt so "stoved up" during storms and cold weather and such. Then she dropped another bomb: "You've got a bad shoulder, too, that right?"

Okay, that did it. I started backing away from her, conscious of performing some mechanical nodding of my head and maybe stammering some kind of pleasantry—because I have a titanium screw and arthritis in my left shoulder, the consequences of a truck accident more than twenty years ago—and because she had successfully freaked me out.

But as I was walking backwards, the once tiny room started to grow and grow until it was like I was sneaking backwards out of a movie theatre. And she was still talking and not moving at all but her voice seemed to be pacing towards me, her voice looming toward me louder and louder even as I retreated. I didn't dare look at her or her dog anymore but stared instead at the warped and rolling plank floor and glanced from side to side to navigate my way toward the door. The last thing I heard her say was "Mervyn will give you a call," Mervyn being her nephew, the man who I hoped would go overseas and drive trucks for Saudia Arabia or go someplace else so far away that I would never have to run into him or his aunt or her little mannequin dog for the rest of my life. Seemed like it took me a year to find the front door but I did, and when I started up my truck I turned the heater on because I was shaking from the damp cold. Once I was home I was relieved to get into some dry clothes at last.

After changing clothes I checked my phone messages. I had missed Mervyn's call by forty-five minutes . . . exactly the time it took me to drive home from his aunt's house.

Chapter Fifteen

When All Else Fails,
Satan Uses the Telephone

I had a love/hate relationship with the phone. I used to joke with Linda that when Satan really wanted something done right, he used the telephone.

Needless to say, the phone was a vital, largely cost-effective conduit for certain kinds of information that a P.I. could not obtain any other way without either compromising the integrity of an investigation or placing themselves in jeopardy. But thanks to the persistence and obnoxious behavior of telemarketers, P.I.'s found themselves caught in the middle of a mini-arms race of antagonistic telephonic devices that had been designed to frustrate live, unscheduled human telephone conversations at almost every opportunity. Contrary to conventional wisdom, P.I.'s often had to spend a disproportionate amount of time and energy just to make a few successful phone contacts and interviews.

Let me give you a typical example.

It was the week before Thanksgiving 2003 and I was trying to wrap up a premise liability case in which a drunken college student sustained serious head injuries after allegedly walking off a fraternity house retaining wall during a party. The case was proving to be an exasperating one, as the task of tracking down and interviewing college students before a holiday break was like trying to catch a bunch of black kittens in the dark. But I only had two witnesses remaining out of the fifteen potential witnesses I had previously identified for interviews.

So I was sitting at my computer, drafting the completed witness interview summaries and waiting for the remaining two witnesses to call me back. I had two days in which to finish my report. I had saturated the answering machines, voicemails, and emails of the reluctant witnesses. I had hoped that they would either feel flattered or annoyed by a private investigator's persistent attention. Either way, I was betting that they would call me that night.

I was listening to the tape-recorded interviews and typing away furiously when the phone rang. Caller ID read a Marion landline phone number and phone listing: "Chester Byrd." Name didn't register in connection with the college case. Phone number didn't match either the cell phones or landlines associated with my two witnesses. I picked up the phone anyway.

"Brian Lee Knopp - Investigator."

A small quavering voice darted out of the phone.

"Hello. This is Maggie Byrd. I don't know how long I can talk--I might have to call you right back—but I wanted to know how much you charge to follow somebody."

"Well, Miz Byrd, is this regarding a marital situation?"

"Yes. See, it's my son—well, really his wife, my daughter-in-law. I think she's cheatin' on him and—oh, I've got to go, I'll call you right back!"

Click.

Huh. Well, back to work.

I returned to drafting the interview summaries. After fifteen minutes or so, the phone rang. Chester Byrd again. I hesitated before answering, deciding whether to let it ring through to the voicemail.

I was never inclined to pick up a domestic case, and I certainly didn't need the headache then—I was swamped. And this woman sounded like she was price shopping. But she sounded elderly and either frail or scared or both. Maybe she'd go away after I gave her the sticker shock of my $50 hourly rate and the $1000 minimum retainer. Maybe I could refer her to somebody else.

I decided to pick up the phone.

"This is Brian Lee Knopp."

She was back, still talking slightly above a whisper, and with great haste.

"Yes. This is Maggie Byrd—I'm the one who called you before about wantin' somebody followed?"

"Yes, Miz Byrd. You wanted to know how much I charge for following somebody—what we call domestic surveillance?"

"Yes."

"My hourly rate is $50, and I require a signed contract and a $1000 initial minimum retainer. Depending on the facts or circumstances surrounding this matter, the total cost could be much more."

"Yes, I understand. Well, it's like I said—I think Natalie, my daughter-in-law, is cheating on my son. And she just had their baby—my grandson, Nathaniel—only sixteen months ago, and here she is, staying out late at night after work and all—she's a waitress at Swiss Valley restaurant, just off the Parkway—and she's been fighting with Luke about this and that, aggravatin' him something turrible when he comes home from work—oh, and she's changed her working schedule, too, thinking that she can fool me about what she's up to. But she works late at night and leaves Nathaniel with one of her girlfriends while she's supposed to be out shopping or running errands in the day but I think she's seeing this fellow she works with during the daytime, too, because people have seen her

94

driving around without Nathaniel. Ardella saw her—that's Ardella Fender, she's my cousin—she saw her take out Nathaniel's little car seat and hide it in the trunk of her car one time. I am worried sick about it all—don't you think that it sounds like she's doing him dirty? I think it does—and I want—oh la! My husband's back—I'll have to call you right back."

Click.

When she hung up, the dial tone indicated that someone had called me while I was listening to Maggie Byrd. I checked my voicemail, and—shit, it had been one of my key witnesses, possibly *the* key witness! She left a message that said she would be going out for the evening in about a half hour, but that I could call her at her apartment or cell phone later on.

I called the apartment number but it was busy. I made two more calls a couple of minutes apart, but the line was still busy. I called her cell phone and left a message for her to call me right back. I stopped working on the witness interview summary and began to prepare for her phone interview. I untangled the phone headset and placed it over my ears, stacked the huge case file near the phone and pulled out the police report, pulled up several other witness interviews summaries on my computer, and checked my digital tape recorders to make sure they were working and had enough recording time left for a possible lengthy interview.

I pondered the upcoming interview, trying to anticipate whatever witness reluctance or conversational obstacles that might arise and figuring out how to overcome them. About five minutes later, the phone rang. My eyes flashed eagerly towards the caller ID, which I had buried with my case documents. I lifted the heap of papers and saw—*What?*

Chester Byrd a/k/a Maggie Byrd.

I let her call ring through to my voicemail. Computer clock read 20:40 hrs. Maggie would have time to call me back before it got too late.

I didn't want to miss my big call. In fact, I was quite anxious to get my witness while she was still at home. I did not want to interview her at length while she was on her cell phone, because her testimony might be compromised by the very mechanics of cell phone usage: weak signal or poor reception; being distracted by trying to simultaneously drive and recall a traumatic event; receiving audience response or influence from individuals who were listed as adverse witnesses in this case and who may be within earshot of her conversation.

I called my witness' cell phone. No answer. I left another message. When I hung up, the dial tone reminded me that someone had left a message.

I was pretty sure that Maggie Byrd had left the message.

She did leave a message. But as I discovered later to my dismay, so, too, did the second of my important witnesses. I hadn't checked the caller ID for that call, and I hadn't retrieved the voicemail in order to discern that a second call had come through—because I didn't want to tie up the phone by retrieving voicemail. I would have missed the call for my first witness, was my thinking. But I didn't find out about the second witness calling me until . . . .

95

Deedle deedle deedle!

Uh-uh. Please no.

I cut my eyes toward the Caller ID unit.

Maggie Byrd again.

Don't pick up.

I didn't pick up.

In fifteen minutes, my first important witness would, according to the message she had left me earlier, be heading out to eat or party or see a movie. And when she did, I would miss out on a timely interview opportunity.

I called the witness's landline and *Hot damn!* it rang. But I got her answering machine! I left a terse message, reminding her that I was trying to call her before she left and before I closed my office for the night. Out of my innate stubbornness when it came to playing phone tag, I called her cell phone and she answered! But before I could get through the obligatory formalities of the conversation, she advised me her cell phone's battery was about to croak—not sure if she had a minute left—and that her girlfriends had arrived to whisk her out for pizza, but could I call her back around 10 or 10:30 PM, if that was not too late?

I told her absolutely yes I could, and I hung up with a sense of accomplishment. One almost down, one left to go.

I checked my voicemail. First there was Maggie Byrd's mouse squeak of a message about wanting to call me from another phone so she could talk without her husband interfering.

Then I heard the second message from my second witness, who had called me from a cell phone, telling me that he'd call me back when he got home in about an hour.

Excellent!

I felt good about the possibility of completing my two interviews tonight. So good, in fact, that when the phone rang, I did not bother checking the caller ID before punching the headset button and answering.

"This is Brian Lee Knopp."

"Mr. Kanupp—it's me, Maggie Byrd."

I suppressed a groan. At least she wasn't whispering this time.

"Yes, Miz Byrd, I'm sorry that I couldn't get back to you sooner, but do you mind if I ask you why you can't talk about this matter with your husband around?"

"Oh, it's just that he doesn't want me to get involved in Luke's and Natalie's affairs—I can't let him find out. And Luke is just like his father—just easy-going, doesn't want to rock the boat, minds his own business—all that poor child does is work and sleep, bless his heart. The way he sees it, things will all work out, and he doesn't want me to worry about it. But it's a mother's right to worry! And I'm Nathaniel's Mamaw, and it is my business—I can't sleep for worrying about what his momma might be up to!"

"Yes m'am, I understand. But is it you or your son who will actually be hiring me or some other investigator?"

"Oh, I will be hiring you. I don't want my son to know anything about it, neither. I've got some money saved up, not much, but it would be worth every penny—do you think it will actually cost the whole $1000? It could cost less, couldn't it? I don't think it will take that much . . . I just know she's seeing that boy from work, because the other day she slipped out and said the name Chris instead of Luke, you know, she told me she had to get off the phone because Chris might be calling, then she said Luke real quick to cover up, you know—if we could just catch her, just one time, then—Oh-oh, Mr. Kanupp, I have to put more change in the payphone . . . click!"

Maggie Byrd had flown.

Payphone?

While I awaited Maggie Byrd's renewed payphone call, I tried to sort out the mess she was in.

Grandmother wants to hire me to get the goods on daughter-in-law.

Sounds like she might be angling for custody of the infant grandchild if her son's marriage breaks up over infidelity.

Doesn't want her son to know anything about it—but what will she do with the evidence?

If she's already quibbling about my costs, will she hire a divorce attorney for her son?

Will her son even go through with the divorce, once he's confronted with the bad news?

Daughter-in-law won't lose custody of an infant child on infidelity alone. If Maggie Byrd isn't sleeping well now, wait until the disapproving husband, the overworked son, and the outraged and humiliated daughter-in-law—all find out that Mamaw hired a P.I. And since she called me long distance, her husband might find out about it before I even finish the assignment, if he looks at the phone bill at all. . . .

More than an hour had gone by. Apart from shuffling papers, waiting on phone calls, and contemplating the woes of the enigmatic, persistent Maggie Byrd, I had done little else.

Deedle deedle deedle!

I shoved the stack of papers off the caller ID, and saw Marion, NC exchange. I assumed Maggie Byrd was calling from the payphone again (this incident occurred before payphones were identified as such by caller ID units). I ignored it, letting it ring through to voicemail. Just as I started to regain my thoughts about the witness interview summary that I had set aside earlier, the phone rang again.

It was a Marion exchange again, but a different number than what had come up minutes before. I was puzzled.

I pushed the headset button and answered the phone and . . . *Aaah!*

"Mr. Kanupp? It's me, Maggie Byrd again."

"Well, Miz Byrd, we might get through a whole phone call tonight, or we might not. What do you think?"

"Oh la, I know, it's pretty frustrating. You can't hardly find a working pay-phone nowadays. And they're so expensive."

"Did you call me just a couple of minutes ago?"

"No. Well, I guess I might have. I started to call but I had run out of change, and had to go to the store, and while I was there I picked up a few Stouffer's dinners for Luke, poor child. Natalie don't even hardly cook no more—it's pitiful, I tell you what . . . ."

Who called then?

My second witness had called, that's who.

His "home" turned out to be in Marion. He was a college student living in Cullowhee, in Jackson County, and when he had said he was "on his way home," it hadn't occurred to me that when he had called on a cell phone that he was on a two-hour drive to his "home" in McDowell County, where Marion was located. If I hadn't been so distracted by all the Byrd calls, I would have double-checked his home address that I had somewhere in the pile of papers slumped over by the phone.

I had just blown off my second important witness. But I didn't find that out until, a half an hour later, I had finally succeeded in interrupting Maggie Byrd's softly-spoken bluestreak of domestic woe.

I called my first witness. I got the answering machine.

I called my second witness. I got the answering machine.

It was now 22:00 hrs. Too late to call a witness who was at home with parents. Since my first witness had advised me to call her after 22:00, I did. I called her three more times up until 23:00 hrs. Answering machine only.

In almost three hours, I had finished only one witness interview summary. I had failed to interview my two important witnesses. And Maggie Byrd never did hire me.

I hoped little Nathaniel was going to be okay.

Chapter Sixteen

Mobile Surveillance and
The Day of The Beast

The irony was crippling. I had moved to the mountains to live on a farm far away from city life so I could live a healthier life. I took up an unconventional livelihood to escape office treachery and confinement. And damned if still didn't spend most of my workaday life sitting in a motor vehicle.

When I was so imprisoned, whether driving or parked—I had fantasies. No, not *those* kinds of fantasies. They were too distracting.

No, I mean I had the kind of wish-fulfillment fantasies a weary P.I. might have had. Like dreaming about the perfect mobile surveillance assignment.

My perfect mobile surveillance assignment would combine all the best features of the most successful surveillance efforts that I had actually conducted in the past.

The perfect fantasy surveillance assignment would go something like this.

I wake up early, yet still feeling refreshed after my ten hours of sleep. I am excited about today's surveillance subject because I know the subject is driving a flashy red car with a radio station bumpersticker prominently displayed on her rear window. I couldn't lose her even if she pulled into a car lot selling only identical red cars. The subject is young, preoccupied with her cell phone, and therefore fairly oblivious to her surroundings. She drives erratically but more or less at the given speed limit.

Her marital home is in a trailer park located at the bottom of a hill, with only one entrance/exit, and her trailer can be seen via binoculars at a distance of over a mile.

My perfect surveillance partner is a female P.I. between the ages of thirty-five to fifty-five, who looks motherly and sympathetic but drives like Dale Earnhardt. She has superb camera skills, ample street-smarts, people-pleasing ways and enough moxie to handle any Oh Shit! moments that may occur. But more importantly, she has enough innate caution and foresight to anticipate Oh Shit! moments and avoid them.

Our vehicles are rented so the license plates cannot be traced to us. Our windows are sparkling clean; our radios are fully-charged and have a strong signal no matter where we drive. And when we get separated beyond radio range, our cell phones still work flawlessly despite the lack of cell towers in the mountains and in spite of the interference posed by the typical low cloud ceiling here.

The day is pleasantly warm, dry, and cloudy, with good overcast lighting. No searing heat, no sunlight daggers stabbing across your cameras' lenses and obliterating your shot. No rain to fog windows or slick streets to fool the cameras' autofocus with reflected images. I have a pursuit camera on board my rental car: a 6-inch video camera hooked to a 24-hour real time VCR. The camera is hidden inside a Kleenex box velcroed to the dash, and the whole system runs off of a golf cart battery. As long as the subject is in front of my vehicle and within six car lengths, everything she does will be recorded. The rental car has huge side view mirrors; the latter will come in handy when I am deliberately turned around to avoid the subject's scrutiny, but still filming her nevertheless with my handheld camera faithfully capturing her reflection in the mirrors.

In the course of the surveillance, we will follow the subject's meanderings across town and naturally we will lose her briefly when she runs a yellow light and turns onto a side street. But no worries, because I know from experience that side street is the preferred route used by locals going to Wal-Mart and the shopping mall area. So I don't sweat it, no, I don't even swear about it. I just press the stopwatch feature on the cheap digital watch that I have strapped to the steering wheel, and note the time visual contact was lost. The stopwatch acts as a gauge of just how gone our subject might be. If we do not re-establish visual contact in fifteen minutes or so by crisscrossing an ever-widening circle beyond the area in which the subject was last seen, we have probably lost her. I radio my partner and tell her to head to Wally World and begin cruising the parking lot. I continue along what I think is or was her most likely direction, scanning the side streets and driveways for the red vehicle. Then the radio crackles to life to tell me that my partner has found our subject in the Wally World parking lot, and she advises that she will follow the subject inside. I tool on over towards Wally World and find a good vantage point for picking up the subject once she leaves the store—a car wash across the street. I film the subject emerging from the store, flinging her purchases into the backseat and trunk of her car, and driving away from the store and all the way to what will turn out to be her lover's apartment.

My partner and I set up in the apartment complex. She will remain in her vehicle; I will be hiding inside a boxwood bush. The night is chilly but my light-weight camo suit is warm enough. The apartment complex is quiet. There are only a few tense moments when dogwalkers go by and their charges snuffle about the boxwood and send their streams of "Pee-Mail" for other dogs to read. But only an hour or so into the evening, an open kitchen window with good back-lighting and no curtains provides the money shot: there's our subject both cook-ing supper for and kissing the other woman in her life. For domestic infidelity, one needs to prove inclination and opportunity. We now have both.

We stay for a few more hours and record the duration of the visit. Around midnight, I radio my partner and tell her we're done, and give her the location of the meet afterwards. Parked in our respective vehicles in the deserted mall park-ing lot, my partner hands me her videotape and surveillance notes as we exchange our perfunctory sardonic congratulations:

"Well, that's that. Another one bites the dust, hey hey."

"Yep. I'll go back before dawn and stay there until I get her driving out, and that'll prove the overnight stay. Dunno if hubby's gonna shit or shine when he hears about the Missus' latest little walk on the *wild* side."

When mobile surveillance went well, it was a ballet danced with steel. After all the hiding, maneuvering, triple-guessing and angling for photo opportunities was done and the money shots obtained, my mood changed from black and white into glorious Technicolor, just like in the *Wizard of Oz*. My heart sang and my clients jumped with joy—okay, they usually didn't jump with joy, but at best they were grimly satisfied—and the pocketed money fairly vibrated with contentment over a job well done.

But when mobile surveillance went badly, it was an ugly beast.

* * * * * *

That was not the day and not the way to be pushing things.

But there I was, pushing it. I had the rented black Mitsubishi Galant side-ways, going 60 mph down the 25 mph entrance ramp before I straightened out into my own blue-white squall of smoking rubber. And then I floored it, my eyes darting only sporadically at the speedometer. All the potential bad news I needed to see at the time was up ahead of me, anyway.

My surveillance subject was speeding away somewhere in the distance. She was last observed traveling west on I-40 and approaching the Morganton area and its four exits, all of which are located within a two mile area. Once she turned off the interstate, she would vanish in the heavy holiday traffic just as easily as she could disappear in the surrounding maze of rural two lanes.

55 . . . 65 . . . 75 . . . 85 mph . . . .

I was hypnotized by the risks before me and numbed by the nonstop mental calculations of those risks.

I was propelled beyond reason by the adrenaline rush that pushed any misgivings and all the laws of Murphy, physics, traffic, and karma combined—right out the tailpipe of the speeding sedan.

I could see The Day of the Beast happening before my rapidly darting eyes. And there didn't seem to be a damn thing I could do about it.

It had been a last minute worker's comp surveillance assignment from a long-term client during the Christmas Holiday back in 2003. The assignment was to set up outside of the subject's home near Valdese, tail her to her doctor's appointment at 14:00 hrs in Morganton, then follow her when she left the doctor's office, and see what her activity level was afterwards. That meant a half-day surveillance, two hours travel time. Not worth it. I talked the client into letting me set up at 08:00, in case the subject did outdoor chores or ran errands, shopped for Christmas presents, or maybe performed an under-the-table job like cleaning houses—prior to making her doctor's appointment. I also convinced the client that it would take two P.I.'s to make the surveillance effort worthwhile. It would definitely take two agents to follow her on the meandering rural roads as well as in heavy holiday traffic. My preliminary due diligence on the location and configuration of the subject's rural home revealed that it was located at the end of a cul-de-sac, and P.I.'s don't like cul-de-sacs. At best, a single P.I. would fail to adequately or discreetly monitor her home activities, or fail to track her departure from the home and follow her through the maze of country roads without being so on top of her that she would know she was being followed. At worst, the lone P.I. might be detected by an irate husband or concerned relative or neighbor and become trapped in the cul-de-sac, blocked in by a vehicle, or even assaulted.

As it was, I had to scramble the night before to find last-minute backup. The next day, I met up with my backup at 07:30, and set up out outside the subject's home at 08:00.

At 08:30, my backup had radioed me about an urgent need to "take care of something" and left his surveillance position.

At 08:45, the subject popped out of her house. I filmed her while she vigorously scraped off her frosted car windows, carried out the trash, and then started her blue Chevy Lumina and let it warm up for a few minutes. I frantically tried to summon my backup. The subject was getting ready to leave, and my partner had been positioned to follow her once she left her dead-end road. I was parked over on an adjacent hillside, off the side of the road, more than half a mile away, in order to film her activities around the home without getting picked off, and to have enough high ground to see which way she would turn at the blind T-road intersection located at the bottom of her road.

At approximately 09:00, she had hopped in her now toasty warm car and Z-

O-O-M-E-D away. I fought the urge to panic.

Fuck! Faked out and far away . . . is no way to play, José!

I tossed the camera and tripod behind the seat, tore off my screening mesh from its velcro anchors, and roared away to try and catch her. By the time I wound my way down from my vantage point and caught sight of—*O merciful P.I. God willing!*—her blue car zipping along the main road, heading for the interstate, she was almost two miles ahead of me.

My backup was silent and missing in action.

But that was not what brought forth the Beast.

No. All that simply constituted a bad moment. And bad moments were frequent, inescapable features of the world of mobile surveillance. With some grace under pressure, good instincts, tenacity, and enough gas in your vehicle, bad moments were quite often retrievable situations. Working under my normal operating procedures, I usually would not blame my backup's ill-timed bathroom break any more than I could my subject's unexpected early morning enthusiasm and her NASCAR driving techniques. Just the way it went sometimes.

The Day of the Beast was different, changing everything utterly. When the Beast appeared, all bets were off. Summoned from beyond the chasms of time and technology that separated the modern from the primitive, The Beast emerged with all primal bones and flint and animal hides intact.

The Beast loved the hunt. The Beast loved furious motion and relentlessness. The Beast hated when obstacles stood in its way.

In the eyes of The Beast, the subject of my worker's comp investigation had changed. She was no longer just some forty-year-old woman who drove with a lead foot in spite of her alleged severe carpal tunnel syndrome, neck pain, and additional left arm neuropathy and radiculitis stemming from a slight herniated disk at C-6 that she supposedly suffered when a handtruck at work loaded with spools of embroidery yarn flipped back and popped her in the chin.

No. Absolutely not.

She was now the embodiment of every unsatisfied hunger, every elusive goal, every raw deal, every bullshit situation, every false or fleeting reward in my life.

And this time, with The Beast's help, she/it/they would not get away with it.

The hunter had changed, too. I was no longer a deliberate and exacting private investigator who had hitherto gained notoriety among his peers for being a knitpickingly thorough researcher and a painstaking planner. I was certainly not regarded as an impulsive, reckless "cowboy" when it came to mobile surveillance.

But the Beast took over. I did not know who I was any longer. My identity and The Beast's single-minded focus on its prey had become one.

This much was conjectured, though: I was perched precariously on a fool's throne, surveying my dizzying domain, the imminent destruction of which hung in hairsbreadth balance between gross negligence and wanton criminality. First driving 85 in a 60 mph zone, then at least 70 in a 30; passing on double yellow; passing on the shoulder; hurtling past *My God!* The North Carolina School for the *Deaf!* All the while, my vision swarmed with obstacles in my way.

And this much was certain: I was *not* having fun. My true identity temporarily misplaced, I was nevertheless still dimly aware of the far remove between Me Now and Me Way Back Then, when I used to enjoy the typical brainless teenage pastime of rocketing along at 100 mph in almost two tons of deadly steel, the roar of the V-8 engine harmonizing with the soaring guitar leads coming out of the car's stereo, the heavy metal music urging me and my primer-spotted muscle car onward to glory.

The nightmare had happened. I had joined with The Beast. And at $45 an hour, during the Christmas holiday, I had joined far too cheaply.

Worst of all, I was acting the hypocrite, exhibiting just the kind of recklessness I would not tolerate from the subcontract P.I.'s I hired for surveillance. I mean, it was all right there in #4 of my Surveillance Code of Conduct form that I had drafted for my subcontractors:

#4) You will not endanger the subject, the subject's family, the public, your fellow investigators, or yourself by driving recklessly or aggressively while following the subject.

Surveillance is basically a way of gathering evidence, whether as part of the informal discovery process for litigation or as part of an insurer's anti-fraud program. Precedents and rules derived from case law and the North Carolina Rules of Civil Procedure govern the proper collection and admissibility of evidence. If a P.I.'s job wasn't difficult enough already, trying to keep up with and conforming to the niceties of these dictates while out in the field would drive anyone to distraction.

For me, mobile surveillance was like being in a submarine. I was quietly submerged in the hunter's mind frame of expectant boredom for hours on end, deep in the insulated depths of my vehicle, surrounded only by electronic equipment and disembodied electronic voices.

Then all hell would break loose. Adrenaline intensified my awareness but narrowed it to tunnel vision. Things appeared at once more vivid and less real. Noises were exaggerated, distorted to the extremes of incoherent roars and hushed sibilant sounds. If I was working mobile surveillance alone—always a dicey undertaking—I might not hear a single human voice except my own all day. I could spend entire eight or ten-hour days so obsessed with one moving car and its driver that the rest of the world melted away. Malls and offices and traffic designs became mere background for my pursuit, like props and facades for movie sets.

There was something about mobile surveillance gone wrong that summoned the Beast like no other investigative activity ever could. There were some mitigating circumstances to this altered demonic state, however. More likely than not, a P.I. conducting mobile surveillance was dehydrated and quite hungry. Eating and drinking would inevitably trigger nature's call, a call that would arrive precisely when your subject was suddenly doing something or going someplace important. The summer heat made the vehicle-bound P.I. meaner than a hornet; winter's cold made us miserable. And certainly the feelings of frustration, confinement, and relative helplessness in the face of other speeding vehicles were common features of our automotive existence, as is the general road rage common to American highways. But these feelings gripped P.I.'s even more strongly because our financial survival depended upon mastering the unknowns of following someone in traffic and photographing them at the same time without getting caught.

Truth told, The Beast had appeared only a few times over the years. When The Beast appeared, memorable, shameful, desperate acts were committed. Rental cars were abused. Various road features such as curbing, shoulders, median strips, and speed limit signs were ignored. While The Beast did not run stop signs and stoplights—the payback was too obvious—it sure made up for lost time in other ways I would like to forget.

It was a very good thing for all concerned that the microphone jacks on P.I.'s videocameras were plugged to block out sound, as it was considered an invasion of privacy to have pictures and sound while videotaping claimants. And a better thing, still, that our dictaphones were turned off or later purged of the incriminating commentary that too often accompanied a tricky pursuit.

But if you were a fly trapped on the inside window of my pursuit vehicle—an extraordinary fly who could also hear my thoughts as well as my vocalized complaints and radio chatter—this is what that Day of the Beast sounded like:

"UNIT 1, THIS IS UNIT 2, DO YOU COPY?"

Maybe I should stop . . . never gonna catch he. And there' what, maybe 200 identical blue Chevy Luminas to look for in Morganton? And if I do catch up to her, at 90 mph she'll see me zoomin' up at behind her like a bad dream and know something's up.

C'mon backup—get off the crapper and assist.

Uh-oh. Was that a trooper? No. Whew!

"Ahhh, you loser! You pulled out right in front of me. . . Oh, now you want to be Safety Sam and belly-crawl, is that it? You were in such a hurry to pull out right in front of me . . . to take a nap? Idiot!"

"UNIT 1, THIS IS UNIT 2, ARE YOU STILL 10-7?

"UNIT 1, 10-13 YOUR STATUS?

"UNIT 1 DO YOU COPY?"

Why does my backup have the urge to take a dump immediately but he spends a half hour to get rid of it? Sending lab samples? What?

"What the—NOW WHAT ARE *YOU* DOING ????"

My God! Eddie Munster! That was Eddie Munster! Fuck me, Eddie Munster just came across the center line at me in a red Dodge Ram pickup, I swear!

Wouldn't THAT suck, getting killed in a head-on with Eddie Munster?

"UNIT 1, THIS IS UNIT 2, DO YOU COPY?"

"UNIT 1 – DO YOU COPY?"

Brian! Just quit. Not worth it. It's starting to rain and everything. . . just not your day today. And if you blow a tire at this speed . . .

"UNIT 2, THIS IS UNIT 1, YOUR 10-2 GO AHEAD."

Ah. About damn time . . . .

"10-4, UNIT 1, I AM IN PURSUIT SOUTHBOUND 64, NEED ASSIST ASAP—STANDBY, I'M 10-6 . . ."

What's this guy in front of me stopped for? C'mon old man . . . .

"C'mon Dad. C'mon, Grandpa."

Is that guy alive? Did he stroke out? Why is he stopped there for so long? There's no traffic . . .

"C'mon Papaw! C'mon Methuselah motherfucker—just go! Go! GO! Some time today, old man! GOOOO! JUST TURN! TURN THE WHEEL! TURN WHEEL, APPLY GAS . . . SAME AS THE MODEL T, REMEMBER? GO! GOOOO!"

"Gotta go! Ready or not, Mr. Greenjeans, here I come . . . you got people behind you . . . JUST. TURN. DAMMIT!!!"

"UNIT 2, THIS IS UNIT 1, I'M 10-8 NOW, WHAT IS YOUR 20?"

"10-4 ON YOUR STATUS, UNIT 1. I'M STILL SOUTHBOUND ON 64, JUST PASSED SALEM CHURCH ROAD—SUBJECT'S VEHICLE IN SIGHT, ¼ MILE LEAD, DRIVING AT HIGH RATE OF SPEED—STAND-BY FOR . . . ."

Yikes!

Where did she come from?

Hmmm. That lady in the Geo Prism veered off the road—that's not good. Hope she didn't get my plate and call it in . . . I shouldn't have cut her off like that— this piece of shit rental car steers like a shopping cart! But hell, she was digging in her purse and talking on her cell phone instead of watching traffic. She should have known better . . . only desperate P.I.'s are allowed to multitask like that on the highway.

OKAY UNIT 1, I'M BACK—TRY TO CATCH UP, REPEAT, TRY TO CATCH UP. IF I CATCH HER I'LL BE RIGHT ON HER AND I'VE HAD TO EXPOSE MYSELF REPEATEDLY BY PASSING TRAFFIC ON THE TWO-LANE WHILE TRYING TO CATCH HER"

"10-4, UNIT 2, I'M 10-17 . . . AND I'VE GOT YOU IN SIGHT—STANDBY . . . ADVISE THERE'S A TEAL GEO PRISM OFF THE ROAD IN FRONT OF ME, WHITE FEMALE DRIVER GETTING OUT OF VE-HICLE . . . LOOKS UPSET . . . KNOW ANYTHING ABOUT THAT?"

"NEGATIVE, UNIT 1 . . . " the Beast lied.

Chapter Seventeen

Paint It Black...and Leaf Colored: Rural Surveillance Expert

Over time, I fell into the niche of a high-risk rural surveillance specialist, tracking down and videotaping disability cheats who had vanished into the mountains. These individuals received monthly worker's compensation or disability payments that resulted from an injury settlement. More often than not, they also continued to work at any number of underground cash economies hidden in the woods: logging, landscaping, ginseng and galax poaching, moonshining, methamphetamine production, marijuana growing, vacation retreat caretaking, etc.

So right out of the box, these were typically very suspicious folk. That these subjects had usually foiled one or more previous surveillance attempts conducted by other P.I.'s only reinforced their hyper-vigilance and raised the stakes. They took their benefit money and purchased radio frequency scanners to pick off P.I.'s radio chatter; they used highly-sensitive parabolic dish microphones and heat-seeking "game finder" tracking devices to scan the woods before exerting themselves beyond their disability rating. Or they went low-tech and dangled fishhooks at eye level, set spring-steel bear traps, or employed teams of dogs, the greatest intruder-detection devices ever invented.

It became a game to them. A real hoot. They were hunting the hunter. Hunting was in their blood, and they played the game with deadly seriousness. As I did, too.

For me, these cases were an inspired necessity. I was willing to do them and I did them effectively. I was better off skulking in the dark forest and not locked down in an office, surrounded by electronic devices, hoping the phone would ring and hating when it did.

I worked these cases alone. P.I. work in general and rural surveillance in particular just doesn't delegate very well. There were too many variables and too few opportunities to communicate all that needed to be done when a twig snapped or a rock kicked loose or a hunting dog set his nose towards you. Furthermore, most P.I.'s were appalled by the prospect of leaving the security of their vehicle to enter a potentially hostile *natural* environment without a full SWAT team backup waiting just beyond the rise for the signal. This reluctance often confounded me, inasmuch as so many P.I's boasted of being avid hunters or having elite military experience with reconnaissance units, wilderness navigation and survival courses, sniper training, etc. I thought they would jump at the chance to go play in the woods again. But there were no takers.

Finally, these types of cases arrived too few and far between to truly specialize in them and consequently avoid doing the jack-of-all-trades assignments that a P.I. in my area had to accept in order to survive.

I would trek up and down the mountains all day long, loaded up with gear: video cameras, tripods, binoculars, extra videotapes, extra camera batteries, canteens, micro-cassette recorder, camouflage netting and a military sniper covering commonly referred to as a Ghillie suit. I took clear, convincing video without trespassing on the subject's property, without violating the subject's reasonable expectation of privacy. For hours I sat quietly without moving, in every kind of weather. I didn't talk on a cell phone or two-way radio every twenty minutes, didn't listen to a distracting (and usually illegal) radio frequency scanner. I went without eating or drinking for hours, and without falling asleep in the peaceful woods.

Most importantly—I did all of that and did not get caught.

And if I had?

Suppose that there was only one thing in the way of your fraudulent enjoyment of monthly disability benefits for life.

And that one thing was some lone fool on the hill, in the woods, with a camera, and his film spinning 'round, threatening to spoil everything.

And there was no one else around.

What would you do? What wouldn't you do?

You who have watched countless hours of action-packed blockbuster movies, televised extreme sports, "reality" police shows, outdoor adventure specials, historical docudramas of combat operations—what could I tell you about my experiences in the woods?

Would it be enough to tell you that I enjoyed these assignments beyond words, beyond any monetary recompense I received? Would you understand that they were at once tranquil and nerve-wracking, quiet and deafening, restorative and exhausting?

Would you even want to know about the hardest part of these gigs?

Do you suppose it was how accountable I had to be for every uncertain moment of my day?

Do you imagine it was the painstaking planning, the property records searches, the long hours tracking and profiling the claimant, the stealthy wilderness navigation skills required to just arrive at and then return from the assignment itself?

Do you feel that it would have been the fatigue, the dehydration, the hypothermia, the heat exhaustion, the intense focus? Or maybe all the ticks, chiggers, briars, spiders, or snakes? Or the errant cattle that nearly drowned me with their piss or almost stepped on my head before they realized what I was and then bolted in panic, their heavy bodies crashing through the woods and thus communicating my presence with almost loudspeaker effectiveness: "LOOK OUT EVERYBODY! SOMETHING WEIRD IS IN THESE WOODS!"

No, it was none of those things.

Please believe me in your heart when I tell that the hardest part was always this: to keep from standing up and shouting "YOU'RE BONED! YOU'RE BONED! YOU STUPID SHIT! I GOT YOU!" when I captured the claimant blowing his lifetime disability benefits by repeatedly lifting something heavy like an engine block or woodstove.

Chapter Eighteen

The Phoenix and the Dung Beetle:
Forensic Dumpster Diving
and Garbage Grabs

T he business cards of private investigators, like everything else in their world, can be highly deceptive.

Struggling sole proprietors and desperate husband and wife teams hide behind monikers that promise abundant resources: Global Analysis Inc.; Full Spectrum Intelligence Agency; Preferred Intelligence Group; Johnson & Associates; Platinum Private Eyes. Ex-highway patrolmen and former Marines borrow heavily from the mythos surrounding government spy agencies to imbue their otherwise unremarkable domestic surveillance operations: Defcon Agency; C I A – Confidential Intelligence Agency; Semper Fi Spy; Cyberspace Sleuths; The Stratintel Op Group – "We *Specialize* in *All Kinds* of Strategic Intelligence Operations!" Rent-a-cop companies heavily staffed with high school G.E.D. recipients, military or police service wash-outs and tough guy wannabes—let you know just how formidable they were by all the badges, eagles, tigers, flags, handcuffs, weaponry, and other intimidating symbols festooning their cards, just in case you overlooked the testosterone-laden company names: "First Strike Security; Never Surrender Guard Company; American Security Specialists – International; Team Delta Protective Services. Then there are the hundreds of unused Sherlock Holmes caps, magnifying glasses, microscopes, bloodhounds, James Bond knockoffs and Maltese Falcons to deal with.

It is a shame that consumer fickleness and marketing demands prohibit the use of more appropriate iconography to represent the true nature of P.I.'s: bookworms, ferrets, badgers, scorpions, pythons, sticky paper flytraps.

I chickened out from using as my business slogan my idiosyncratic yet heart-felt definition of a private investigator: *A librarian with a license to loiter.* Too much alliteration.

Actually, the perfect symbol for a P.I. should be the phoenix, the mythical bird who keeps recreating itself from the ashes of its own infernal past. Because the truest, most comprehensive answer to the question eternal "How do you become a private investigator?" is this: *You first have to fail at something else.*

I opted instead for the image of a lighthouse, that still lovely but now obsolete beacon of hope, reliability, and forewarning. I must say that the lighthouse turned out to be a telling marketing symbol for a private investigator who had no real nautical experience and who lived and worked some 300 miles from the nearest coast.

Actually, the dung beetle might be the perfect symbol for private investigators. That useful little insect always came to mind whenever I had to go dumpster diving or perform garbage grabs, the two most undervalued talents in the investigative business.

It goes without saying that mining people's trash for information—howsoever legal in certain circumstances—was just plain dirty business.

Dirty business that I didn't mind doing, actually.

It wasn't an everyday kind of gig, thankfully, because there were so many other so-called "cleaner" sources of information. Also, the legal and ethical restrictions governing the collection and use of private garbage were numerous, and the opportunities to admit garbage as admissible and relevant evidence in court were few.

It did challenge me on many levels, though. I have an extremely sensitive nose and an indelible olfactory memory. I am also one of those people who only has to walk by a dirty car to become completely begrimed myself. I hated wearing rubber gloves and am allergic to latex. And worst of all, I have a very weak voyeuristic instinct and a very strong sense of personal privacy—two traits that hamstrung me from the very beginning of my investigative career.

For the practitioner, dumpster diving and garbage grabs appealed to the love of scavenger hunts and puzzles—though the pieces were covered with salad dressing, coffee grounds and much worse.

I think many otherwise decent folks harbor a dormant yet stubbornly resistant strain of juvenile delinquency. We thrill to feverishness when we have an opportunity to legally steal something that supposedly no one wants any more. And there is the green ethic of recycling at work here, always near and dear to my heart: *today's waste may be tomorrow's fraud indictment or collected judgment.*

I first became inured to the stink and stain of garbage during my college years. My board job was collecting garbage for the largest all-male dorm on campus. I had to haul myself and the garbage in a manually-operated elevator by tugging on a wrist-thick, coarse-fibered Manila bullrope which looped around a huge pulley and a friction brake. I would pull my way up to the fourth floor of the dorm and collect that floor's trash receptacle, then work my way down to the ground floor, where I would dump three floors' worth of trash before descending to the basement floor and collecting their discards, finally hauling them back up to the ground floor again.

Every week the trash would contain you name it. Tons of paper and plastic wrappers. Leftovers. Bottles and cans filled with beer, bong water, chewing tobacco spit. Used condoms. Puke-covered and/or shit-stained clothing. The occasional small dead animal signifying a disgusting college prank or secret religious practice.

It was a horrible job but I made the best of it. I wore a paper crown from Burger King on my head and an old fringed curtain over my shoulders. I would show up at the dorm at midnight on Sunday, greeting each floor with the loud reverberating *GONG!* of heavy steel elevator doors flying open like blast doors to the spacecraft in *Star Wars*. My shouted proclamation of "BEHOLD! THE GREAT AND POWERFUL GARBAGE KING IS HERE!" echoed along the hall and up and down the elevator shaft. Then I would step through the doorway and receive the usual hostile welcome of verbal abuse, beer cans, fireworks—whatever they had on hand.

This board job paid the most of any other available, and I made about $40 a month extra just from the deposits on all the cans and bottles. I would also cut out the proof of purchase labels and give them to one of the dorm's housekeepers, who would collect them and turn them in for money and split it with me down the road.

Who could have known that by huddling down every weekend underneath the fitful light of a bare bulb hanging in the garbage collection room and sorting through foulness for extra coin deep into the night, I was unwittingly preparing for my investigative career?

How much unpleasantness would I endure to get the goods on my subject? I've sat in a car for a week, three hours each morning, five hours each night, waiting for someone to toss their Hefty bags into a dumpster. I've jumped inside a fetid dumpster on a summer's night, armed only with a headlamp, heavy gloves, army surplus mechanic's overalls and a pair of long-handled barbecue tongs and a heavy-duty outdoor grill spatula, the latter of which I used to smack rats and cats out of the way. I have sorted through steaming heaps of maggoty garbage to find the paid receipt, the Western Union money transfer, the annotated advertisement section of the newspaper, the pharmacy labels, the expired video rental card, the postcard from Branson, Missouri that advised *looking forward to seeing you up here again in May! Love, Naughty Nurse.* I've begged a private waste disposal contractor to let me wear a safety vest and just ride on the back of a garbage truck to help pick up the trash belonging to an exclusive gated community. I've risked getting attacked by a startled homeless man while I was rummaging around in a dumpster, even though I don't think that particular guy ever looked back, let alone recovered from the shock of encountering a 6-foot tall black rat with one red eye in the middle of his forehead (I was wearing a headlamp with a red lens), a rat that hissed at him: "*Getthefuckouttahere. This is MINE!*"

One sultry summer morning just before daybreak, a small child wearing an oversized Mickey Mouse T-shirt that billowed down around his knees appeared out of nowhere. He started running after me and crying out in a piercing voice as I filched garbage bags from the curbside in front of his condo unit: "MISTER GARBAGE MAN! MISTER GARBAGE MAN!" The little kid disappeared inside his garage for a moment, only to reemerge dragging a broken rocking horse. The riding toy was twice his size and as he struggled with it down the driveway it started bucking and lunging crazily about on rusted springs that emitted a harsh metallic hiccuping sound more appropriate to a drunken donkey. The rocking horse was loud enough to wake up the entire sleeping condominium complex and loud enough to make me slam the truck door shut on my left knee in my haste to flee. I limped for a week. The garbage grab yielded probative evidence: the little boy's mother was hiding a lucrative second income stream and a long-distance boyfriend while continuing to receive alimony, child support, and disability benefits.

I was always nonplussed whenever someone asked me about the strange things that turned up in the trash. How could I tell them the truth?

"So tell me . . . what's the weirdest thing you've ever found in someone's trash?"

Me.

Chapter Nineteen

James Bond Lost in Kudzu

My work never ceased to transform me. At the end of a full day's and/ or night's work, I often found myself only three foot tall, or a thousand years old, or moving about like a sock puppet that somebody had stuffed with sea shells and then stepped on over and over.

Don't get me wrong. As far as P.I.'s went, I was obscenely healthy. I did not smoke, occasionally drank. I was a lean, mean, spying machine. I was easily mistaken for a road biker, a windsurfer, a roofer, a masonry laborer, even as a skinny hippie street kid—and performed passably well at all of those endeavors (don't be fooled about the last one—panhandling was tough work.).

But my workaday worlds coiled about each other, squeezing me between them, squeezing ever more tightly each day.

Around 1999, as my business began to increase, the novelty of being a P.I. began to wear off and the reality of my situation set in. I would have to struggle simultaneously with the worst of two worlds.

First I was toiling away on a frugal, very rugged farm where only accidents and weeds happened quickly; where animals were notoriously early risers and where seasonal chores always needed to be completed precisely during the busiest times of the legal calendar and in spite of fickle mountain weather.

Then I was gone, driving the labyrinthine mountain roads, twisting and turning, climbing and falling, hurtling through the splendid seasonal displays of green tufted velvet, fiery autumnal mosaic, gray tree bones, bluish-white cold. Before my investigative work could even properly begin, there was adversity, there was uncertainty. I had to navigate my way through places like Bugger's Hollow, Bee Log, Doe Bag, Lickskillet, Possomtrot, Upper Pig Pen, Sodom, Hanging Dog Gap, Relief, Loafer's Glory, Lost Cove. Don't get lost. Don't ask for directions. Don't get them curious. Their culture is a car culture, they know everyone by their vehicle, and they never forget a strange one. Drive by once, okay, drive by twice . . . maybe. Third time, never. While driving, I'm dodging the usual unannounced boulder, fallen tree, jumpy deer, fleeing bear, scurrying raccoons, milling hunting dogs with tracking aerials waving, dragging their rifle-toting, orange-hatted handlers through the fog. I would eye river levels and sagging homemade plank bridges. I would sniff the wind for storm fronts. I would be driving at all hours, through every imaginable weather condition, over tooth-rattling hardpan of unpaved backroads, through tire-sucking mud. I had to squeeze inside my beat-up old Toyota pickup because there was Just. So. Much. *Shit* in there, and yet I always feared that I had forgotten to bring something essential. Binoculars, topo maps, real property tax listings, and criminal rap sheets all balanced on my lap, I worked the manual shift while simultaneously checking the battery or recording tape levels on my cameras or tape recorders and peeing into an empty plastic Gatorade bottle. I fought off fatigue and focused on my mission. I was deep inside my multi-tasking reverie in which I would review all of my preparations, choice of tactics, time constraints, investigation expenditure limits, and applicable case law. Yet I was still alert to any signs of relevant information while in pursuit: "DANGER – BRIDGE OUT – DETOUR;" "WATCH OUT—ILL BEES!" "LOST – HERD OF CATTLE!" "STOP RIGHT NOW! HAVE YE BEEN DIPPED IN THE BLOOD OF THE LAMB? IF YE BE NOT SAVED, YE WILL DIE!"

It was daunting, to say the least, to decompress and shift into the farm-chores-are-awaitin' mode again at 05:30 hrs after going to bed only two hours earlier, having just spent the night watching and hearing a hulking bruiser of a father threatening to beat a 3-year-old stepchild—"YOU WANT ME TO WHIP YOUR STINKY? HMM? YOU WANT ME TO WHIP YOUR STINKY? IS THAT WHAT YOU WANT? 'Cause that's just what I'll do. I'll whip your stinky good, HEAR ME?!" —while I was all but helpless to do anything about it because I was paid to be watching and waiting for his neighbor's marriage to detonate upon the arrival of certain brunette in a Dodge Neon bearing the bumper sticker "God Allows for U-turns."

Chapter Twenty

The Winds of Shock

I almost cheered aloud when I saw the sun's tangerine glow just above the horizon on that clear morning in September.

Excellent!

I had taken the day off from P.I. work in order to finish sowing lime and turkey manure on my north-facing pasture. I needed the happiest weather possible for that particular chore. I would be walking up and down and back and forth on steep slopes while carrying a 5-gallon bucket filled with a mixture of lime and manure pellets. The bucket would weigh 40 pounds and the fertilizer mix would be sufficient to sow only a single, ten foot wide swath at a time across the two-acre pasture. I dispersed the mix by dipping my right hand downward while swinging the bucket upward with my left in a combined motion to greet it, then flinging the pellets in a more or less consistent fan-shaped spread as I walked, crossing the pasture a dozen times.

September mornings are usually cloaked in heavy fog and even heavier dew until about 10:00 hrs. My boots get soaked through before I have a chance to do much of anything. The ground moisture definitely compromises my footing on my pasture's steep slopes. But the moisture has rewards that go far beyond growing forage for sheep: it turns the countless spider webs and ground spider funnels into pearled, glistening orbs that give off a frosty white glow against the green velvet sheen of the slick grass.

But all things considered, I was happy for the drier ground on that day.

I went out to work at 07:00. I came back to the house to refill my water bottle at 08:30, and checked my phone messages then. There were none. I went back to work in an even better frame of mind. Beautiful day, no phone calls, I felt good. I worked steadily until my bucket-carrying arm began to elongate painfully out of proportion to the seed-casting arm. This took me up to about 11:00. I had almost finished with the pasture, anyway. Just an hour or so of work after lunch and I would be done.

As I walked back toward the house, my two dogs started whining expectantly, launching their plaintive little cries like missiles to the heart. I took them out of their kennel and we played games for a while until we all just collapsed on the ground and had a free-for-all wrestling match. The dogs were delighted with the anarchic struggle. We formed a rolling pile of sweaty cloth, flesh and fur, wrestling and chewing and grabbing and scrabbling around on the sun-soaked grass. Fragrant patches of mountain mint were crushed during our play. The mountain mint masked the turkey manure smell to me but not to my dogs, and my hands provoked intense snuffling, pawing, and tonguing scrutiny.

This happy heap of dogs and man on a bright day was pure joy, a delight second only to that derived from the marital bed. Keeping the leaping and lunging Blue Heelers at bay, I reflected on my life, and made an inventory of the ways it pleased me now.

I was satisfied with my professional life. I could finally accept or refuse P.I. assignments on my terms, without feeling constantly tossed between the twin horns of financial necessity and professional obligation. I could work rings around my peers when I had to, enduring whatever animosity or adversity presented itself, and still have energy and enthusiasm left over for the farm and rural lifestyle that I dearly loved. I had hurled myself across the digital divide and into cyberspace and featured my business on a website. In spite of myself, I had succeeded in mastering many new electronic sleuthing techniques and consequently increased my versatility and effectiveness as a legal investigator.

I was happy in my personal life. I felt a deep contentment in the quiet little life Linda and I had cobbled together out of the hours we had hidden away from the demands of our working days and nights. Linda's gift for green growing things and my devotion to animals melded us even more closely together; we shared in the endless duties of farm life that brought charm and challenge in equal measure.

And on this gorgeous, quietly productive day that was September 11, 2001, I was just so *grateful* to be working at my rhythm and by whatever grace I could borrow from destiny; to be sitting tired and peacefully under the sun with my best friends, my dogs and I letting our shadows fall where they may.

The dogs heard the sound of the ringing phone coming through the screen door before I did. Their short stiff bat-like ears rotated towards the sound like little satellite dishes. I ran toward the house and jumped inside just as the last ring cleared the call and sent it to my voicemail.

When I walked into my office, my caller ID unit displayed the dismaying fact that I now had *sixteen* messages. All of them but one had been logged between 9 and 10 in the morning. The messages were mostly from friends and family. The call I just missed was from my mother—her fourth call—who was sounding very worried about why I had not responded to her previous three calls regarding the attack on the World Trade Center. Another call had been from a corporate client, who had usually exhibited common sense and restraint. He now wanted to know what kind of semiautomatic pistol he should carry. His final comment: "Well. . . you might laugh at me, but I tell you, if some damn A-rab starts some shit right in front of me, I'll be glad to have something more than my dick in my hands."

There was this Cherokee wise woman—or "Thunder Woman" as the Cherokee call those formidably outspoken and versatile female tribal members—whom I had known for years who lived right down the road from the town of Cherokee, and just off the banks of the Oconoluftee River. She was in her sixties, and she was just incredible. I relied upon her help whenever I needed to locate someone—or to investigate anything at all—on Cherokee tribal lands. She was a midwife, nurse, traditional healer, Chinese food addict, and garrulous story-teller. She knew everybody and seemingly everything that went on in the Qualla Boundary. The descriptive phrase "multidimensional awareness" seemed like New Age twaddle until you watched her simultaneously perform the following: mix Kool-Aid for her grandkids; listen intently to a police scanner for ambulance calls; alternately talk on the phone in Cherokee and speak North Carolinian to several visiting herbalists and one private investigator sitting in her kitchen; and all the while drawing me an eerily prescient and precise diagram of an impromptu squatter's camp set up in Big Cove. The drawing would eventually prove accurate right down to the location of every ramshackle shed, dilapidated camping trailer, mean dog, and fisherman.

"Thar ye go, hon. He'll be fishin' up thar, next to a yeller outbuilding that has tires throw'd on top of the roof. But don't you go 'round askin' about him—you might get in trouble with some of them bandits who stay up thar. When you see him, just tell him who sent you and what you got for him and no pussyfootin' around about it, 'cuz that'll just make him nervous. Best time to talk to Inniuns about anything important is either early of a morning or late of an evening. So you've got plenty of time. We could all go eat Chine-eeze! Hah hah!"

Anyway, I once heard her say: "What you don't see, you cain't remember." She said that to a distraught woman who had called her one day when the woman's brand new house had burned to the ground just hours after they had moved into it. A total loss.

"Honey . . . lissen to Mama Jean now. Just walk away. Okay, hon? Just walk away. Don't even try to *look* at the house . . . it's gone. Forgit all about it. Just git in yer car and drive away from it. There's nothin' to do about it, baby. *What you don't see, you cain't remember.* You'll forget the hurt before you know it. Trust Mama. Inniuns know all about handling the hurt."

I took her advice. For the rest of that September, I deliberately averted my eyes from every TV that even hinted at replaying the image of the aircraft plunging into the towers. I had more than enough violent images to overcome in my life. I didn't need one more to convince me of our species' measureless potential for atrocity.

But in this case, it did not matter what evasive action I took. The winds of shock would eventually sweep down over my mountain home like some exotic storm front from the northeast, the likes of which no one in these parts had ever seen.

I kept trying to revive deep in my flesh the good feeling of that morning, like rekindling the warmth of a campfire burning down in the face of a dead winter night. I tried to hold on to the sunny September day with all of my strength; to hold onto the way my face felt being tickled by the rose petal softness of dog ears and the wet velvet of dog tongues; the way my body felt being buffeted by vigorous and squirming little canine bodies. I wanted to stay in that protected center of my own grounded awareness of that day, an awareness of a simple man working the land as best as he could under the watchful and approving eyes of God and Dog alike.

Within two year's time, both my dogs would be dead. They had been my best little friends for fourteen and fifteen years, respectively. They would each die in my arms on the same date—March 21st—one year and twenty minutes apart from each other. The first day of Spring is now and forever a day of sorrow for me.

Within two year's time, my mother's mind would spin out of control from fear and worry and age. Starting on 9/11, her erratic flights from reality would punch holes through the emotional fabric of my family that time and tears have yet to repair.

Within two year's time, family and business pressures would compel me to quit shearing sheep and sell off most of my own flock. These same pressures would change forever my relationship to my investigative profession.

Things changed slowly at first. Right after the 9/11 attacks, it was strangely business as usual. Some folks seemed sadder than they were used to. The old men who hung out to bullshit each other at the courthouses and country stores, veterans of WWII and Korea, seemed quieter and more weary-looking, acting like men who were suddenly faced with a chore they swore they would never have to do again in their lifetime. But North Carolina is heavily militarized, and as the drumbeats of "America's New War" grew louder, so too did the jingoism, bravado, and rage. "Tell Bin Laden I've been loadin'!" warned the bumper stickers. "Watch what you say" warned Ari Fleischer, and people did. "KILL THE

DIXIE CHICKS!" read the subject thread of a P.I.-only online chat group. Duct tape and sheet plastic disappeared from store shelves. "We Love Our Freedom!" appeared as hand-made signs shoe-polished onto battered windshields of beat-up cars limping along the backroads on their way to factory jobs that would close up within a year and move overseas.

And my job grew more difficult by degrees.

People were becoming more suspicious, more confrontational, less willing to talk about anything but vengeance and with anything less than belligerence. Security guards metastasized from lowly gate-watchers and parking lot attendants to lethal menaces with dreams of shooting the first person who could correctly pronounce "Al Quaeda." My corporate clients turned surly, abandoning concerns for discretion and respect towards surveillance subjects. "So what if he sees you? Park right in front of his house, we don't care. Let him try to file a bad faith claim! I hope he does know we're watching him—that will send a message that we're not messing around anymore."

The private pays began freaking out more than usual—which didn't seem possible, given their usual state of agitation. They wanted to find out who was really behind all the telemarketing calls they received; to know who spilled the antacid powder in their car to make them think it was anthrax; to prove that their spouse was spying on their Internet activity—or to spy on their spouse's Internet activity.

This climate of fear and intimidation intensified as the economy sank. P.I.'s grew hungry and desperate and looked to the reactionary Good Ole Boy machine to help them run over the competition. Rising fears seemed to outstrip even the most exaggerated doomsday scenarios marketed by executive protection ("EP") outfits, and EP business boomed.

The word was out. Homeland Security was a cash cow to be milked. If you didn't get your hands on the teets now, you'd soon be out of business. The message was fear sells. That message had been out for some time, but now it was as unavoidable as a marching band in your garage.

In the chat rooms and online professional listservs, the Good Ole Boys were talking tough and running scared and racing to the bottom all at the same time. They were ostracizing those without police or military cred and kicking to the curb those they found politically suspect. Yet the Good Ole Boys were welcoming the very changes in the industry that would eventually price most of them out of the business.

The demand for turning personal information into a commodity like toilet paper or batteries had been growing for a decade. After 9/11, it exploded beyond reason and control. Information database vendors were cutting P.I.'s throats in two directions: making confidential information available to our larger clients— law firms and corporations—at lower rates than those offered to P.I.'s and yet holding these high-volume end users of this information to much lower standards of accountability than those required of P.I.'s.

The irony was complete. More and more people were doing sensitive records searches without any true accountability at precisely the same time when concerns for the public's safety and privacy were increasing.

The computer and microelectronics industries helped fuel consumer expectations of and the subsequent demand for state-of-the-art gadgetry as the cure-all to investigative and security conundrums. These companies were still smarting after the dot.com bubble burst in 1999 and 9/11 gave them just the marketing push they needed. They allied themselves with commercial data miners and other info brokers and touted complete investigations at the click of a mouse. And their efforts were wildly successful. Clients were more than willing to trade privacy concerns and even accuracy for convenience and initial low operating costs.

And if clients couldn't exactly become their own cybersleuths, they certainly expected the ones they'd hired to have all the high-tech goodies: pinhole cameras, microwave transmitters and receivers, radio frequency grabbers, computer keystroke counters, etc. They wanted it all. They didn't care if the gadgetry was effective or appropriate or even legal. They just wanted stuff, and P.I.'s struggled to satisfy the growing sophistication of their clients' demands. But clients not only expected P.I.'s to have all this new stuff and know how to use it, but also to cost less per hour than a good auto mechanic or plumber. Such unrealistic client demands soon became a familiar part of the post 9/11 landscape.

To me, the most disturbing development immediately after 9/11 was the silence of the women in the profession. I listened with dismay as the thoughtful, impassioned, articulate voices of female investigators—voices that had been growing stronger in professional discussions before 9/11—now seemed to falter and become uncertain or altogether mute. Even worse, some of the more prominent female investigators had flipped and turned into shrill cheerleaders for the increasingly malicious and blinkered thinking that now seemed to govern even the most trivial P.I. topics.

I despaired. The P.I. world had always been dangerously inbred. Now it verged on monoculture. Once there were Good Ole Girls in the profession, there would be no safe place to hide.

Chapter Twenty-One

The Collision of Worlds

My mother had always warned us kids about watching too much TV. And so after watching the 9/11 attacks for the thousandth time, my mother's mind proved itself correct once again and then melted down.

Perhaps the white-hot heat of her curiosity simply burned through her judgment, blurring the boundaries between memory and imagination, melting reality into misshapen, fear-bound creatures only she could see.

Maybe. Or maybe she was just defying her obsolescence and was bored with being old. Maybe she felt that playing perpetual Phantom of the Opera with the plastic, fertile, image-laden theatres offered by both paranoid delusions and the Information Age was much more of a challenge.

The real tragedy, though, was that her delusions were not compelling enough to get her elected to public office, or hired by some defense industry think tank. Instead, they were merely *exhausting*.

What happened?

No one seemed to know for sure. Not the diagnostic manuals, not the psychologists, not the social workers, not the Wiccan priestess my mother kept harassing by phone. All I kept hearing was the word "not." Not Alzheimer's. Not a stroke. Not schizophrenia. Not well. Not sure what's wrong. Not much we can do.

As a P.I., my schedule was not my own. I lived by the clock my clients and my targets kept. Yet somehow I still found the time to work damage control for my mother's delusions. I would answer the polite questions posed by an FBI agent out of Charlotte, by reporters from the local newspapers. The nights I reserved for dealing with complaints lodged with the Asheville Police Department and with the saintly manager of my mother's apartment complex.

The days brought other duties. I would use all of my tracking skills to find her and take her off of Greyhound buses bound for Tijuana. I would unpack her suitcases twice a week; retrieve her boxed belongings—jettisoned because they were contaminated with anthrax or harbored listening devices—from the apartment courtyard; fix her deliberately jammed deadbolt locks for the twentieth time; drive by her apartment almost nightly—either after my daytime work or before my late night work began—in order to search the grounds around her apartment for all those spies, burglars, drug dealers, raped childhood girlfriends, dismembered grandchildren.

One evening, after spending three hours in a prison for a one-hour convict interview, I stopped by my Mom's apartment for a much needed hot shower to wash off the vibe of the dull gray concrete prison and the dull gray concrete prisoners. But instead of getting clean, I spent four hours trying to convince her that while there were indeed such sophisticated electronic eavesdropping equipment that could fit in her nose, her ears, or underneath that mole on her ankle she never noticed before—there was absolutely no reason to believe that either the FBI or the CIA would spend so much money and effort on a seventy-something woman who had only raised children and worked at either janitorial jobs or daycare centers her entire life adult life.

Whenever her dementia became full blown, I would stay with her for days at a time. She would dig her nose and ears bloody to remove the transmitters that were not there; she would attack me verbally because I could not hear the voices that she heard, could not believe the web of impending peril she wove; could not convince her to lay down her arsenal of kitchen knives and pepper spray because I was not a body double imposter, one of many who were after her and her alone.

I was her son. To keep the shreds of peace that still existed between us, I kept buying her Benadryl, chocolate, and menthol cigarettes, all of which she craved hard and loud the minute that snake-eyed look took hold of her. I rented movies from the '30s and '40s and stayed up with her long after she'd fallen asleep.

In the middle of the night there were moments when she asked in a groggy voice "What time is it, Boo-boo?" and it sounded like her and she was using one of her pet names for me and *Oh!* my heart staggered over itself with joy and relief at the return of The Mommy.

It didn't last. The Mommy was gone.

Eventually, I would betray her.

I played along with her most horrific delusional episode and turned it against her for her own so-called "good." I convinced her that the paralegal friend whom I had begged to help me with this final act of treasonous filial love—the act of obtaining a signed and witnessed legal power of attorney that I could present to the hospital in order to initiate her care—was really a female FBI agent specializing in electronic counter-surveillance measures. The FBI agent needed a signed consent form before she could sweep the apartment for listening devices. My mother signed. "Agent Stone" then used a cell phone taped underneath a pager, occasionally beeping numbers to indicate that yes, my Mom's apartment was bugged. I told my Mom to grab a few essentials, because we had to leave immediately after Agent Stone was finished. I told her that I had worked out an ingenious plan to give my mother's pursuers the slip: we would leave with some friends of mine who had quietly parked an ambulance in the apartment complex parking lot. The perfect cover! My mother was ready in seconds: credit card, toiletry kit, a hidden $100 bill (which she would need later on when she tried to bribe the orderlies in the psychiatric unit to let her escape); several tear gas and pepper spray canisters (I removed all but one of these from her on our way out of the apartment).

We made our escape. My mother arrived at the hospital. Mission accomplished.

I stayed with her in her room while she slept a deeply drugged sleep for eleven hours—possibly the first real sleep she had had in weeks. I remained with her up until she was taken to the locked psychiatric unit at almost midnight. The delay was understandable. It was a full moon Friday, and the hospital's ER found my terrified mother far less compelling than the victims of drug overdoses, car wrecks, stabbings and assaults. After they took her to the psych unit, I went back to her apartment and crawled into a fetal ball and exploded into great choking scalding tears. As I lay there alone in the apartment crowded with Mom smells of cigarettes and scented soaps and fabric softener, I began to hear voices, too. One voice in particular inside my head that was not my own.

The voice sounded like my Mom. I think she was saying goodbye.

But she would be back in her apartment in two days, unchanged except maybe better rested. Were it not for $8,000 in medical bills and the gaping hole in my heart, it would be hard to tell that the incident had ever taken place. And yet except for the hospitalization, these "incidents" would occur several times a year for almost three years, right up until her death in 2006.

I was bitter about the experience—but for some of the oddest reasons.

Like how my cover was gone for good. All my efforts towards carefully maintaining a low, innocuous profile emblematic of my profession's utmost discretion and confidentiality were blown away like leaves in one of the fierce thunderstorms my mother liked to walk in while chain-smoking menthol cigarettes and carrying a flashlight.

I became *very* well known around Asheville. But not like Sam Spade or Jim Rockford. No, I was the private investigator whose mother was "that crazy lady."

Most bitter of all was my feeling of failure. I am a man, innately hardwired to protect and defend women at all personal cost, and there was no duty more sacred than to save The Mommy. But the best I could do was to use all of my P.I. cunning to trick her into her fully participating in her worst nightmare.

I must admit, though, that on the surface, my Mom looked . . . *great* for someone who binged on Benadryl, menthol cigarettes, chocolate and coffee while constantly being pursued by assassins, Manchurian candidates, and other henchmen who wanted everyone to think she was a flake so no one would believe her stories.

Whenever I looked into the mirror—I saw a person falling apart.

And I was bitter because I became frightened—incredibly frightened, scared to the quick of my soul—about the hall of endless mirrors I seemed to be entering as I dealt, both professionally and personally, with people whose delusions seemed so bulletproof and oddly sustaining, even profitable. Whereas my reality suddenly seemed so vulnerable, so unwieldy, so unworkable, so debilitating. A private investigator/farmer/shepherd/sheep shearer/writer/elder care provider? Who would try to do all of that? They must be insane.

As the sibling primarily responsible for her care at the time, I spent three years trying to put the puzzle together again, and failed. No, I "**FAILED!**" in heavy leaden headlines that fell down and crushed me every time I thought about her.

I **FAILED** at my biggest, most challenging case of "whodunnit"—although a more apt, darkly humorous description would have been "whoisit?."

My mother's case is closed. But it remains unsolved.

Chapter Twenty-Two

The Vodka Boatman

I didn't grow up with any desire whatsoever of being a private investigator. It just seemed to be waiting for me, like a stage locker with my name on it stuffed with masks, cloaks, props, scripts finished and not, all necessary equipment for distracting me and many others from the pain of my unrealized goals: veterinarian, writer, nomadic shepherd, shaman. The gig seemed to be an attractive option against other, more disturbing manifestations of failure. Like unemployment. Like drug addiction. Like prison.

Beyond the fatigue and the worries from the job, there was always that indescribable depletion, that nameless emptiness that came from not being able to talk freely about the day's or night's events with Linda. That was the worst. I didn't tell her because I did not want to compromise my client's confidentiality. And I didn't tell her because I did not want to spread the collateral damage even further.

When I crept home in the middle of the night, the tumult of the day was still roaring in my head. I made my way swiftly and silently through the house, fearing all the while that the jagged smithereens of other people's lives would fall out of me and wake her before I could shut the office door. As I caught sight of her sleeping, of her ear like a perfect seashell peeping through the drifts of her hair—I would stop, spellbound. I was awestruck by how small a thing she was, a slender life raft in a maddened sea. Yet she was my pole star as well, and I would do anything to keep that star undimmed for me.

Even if it meant my silence.

Sure, I could come home and joke with my wife about generalities. I could talk about anyone and anything except my clients and the details of their cases.

But I couldn't tell her about so much. The child abuse photos. The rambling, erratic suicide notes with the weirdly spaced letters and eerie shifts in pronouns and verb tenses, as if the writer had been struggling with another narrator who kept interfering. The festering potential of being trapped far from home on an isolated mountain farm by individuals too frightening to ever be cast in the movie *Deliverance*. The vile threats made by law enforcement officials and the sinuous, almost graceful intimidations whispered by high-profile drug dealers.

Until now, I could never tell her about The Vodka Boatman and his double-barreled shotgun. He was always just the once a week bad dream I mumbled about to her as I got up out of bed in the middle of the night to go read somewhere with all the lights on. Avoiding The Vodka Boatman incident always made me feel unfaithful, made me feel dirty in a way that I had never felt about anything else that I had experienced since our marriage in 1989.

Close on the heels of my **FAILURE!** with my Mom came another far-reaching failure, a moment when all of my heightened sensitivities shut down and my well-honed instincts abandoned me.

It seemed like one morning I woke up with my cat's whiskers cut, my dog's nose plugged and my deer's ears closed. And like all victims of such cosmic pranks, I had no idea that any of this had occurred. There had been no omens. I had broken no shoelaces, spilled no coffee, shattered no mirrors, and spoken no angry words to my wife over the breakfast table. I smilingly went off to work on a pretty day. . . and damned if I didn't nearly get cut in half by the most improbable gun-toting fool I ever suffered to meet in the mountains.

It shook me to my core. And it wasn't the fact that I met up with the wrong end of the gun that spooked me so profoundly, either. Because that had happened numerous times before and, well, hell, you can get a gun pointed at you around here for fishing in the wrong spot.

No, it was the fact that nothing, absolutely nothing, told me that I might meet someone like the Vodka Boatman before I actually did—and by then it was too late. The unreasonably high level of self-confidence that had sustained me all these years vanished at the sight of him. Like a mountain climber who had placed all of his strength and faith in a rock ledge that inexplicably crumbled underneath him, I had only enough nerve left to leave.

The Vodka Boatman was the name I gave to this drunken old geezer who, on a bright crisp fall day, answered my knock upon his trailer door. This tall, wizened man, who looked to be all of eighty-something, had a pasty round head wobbling atop white shiny cables of muscles and ligaments that twitched and bunched like fat worms crawling underneath the scrawny neck. His fading eyes—milky blue stains leaking through sclerotic, Saran-wrapped lenses—peered out over puffy cheeks that were cross-hatched with broken capillaries and odd scars shaped like wads of chewed gum, scars which also covered his slick forehead. He had a short little white chin beard, like Ho Chi Minh's. The Boatman was standing twisted to one side, like someone bracing against a gust of wind. As he filled the doorway, I could smell the booze cooking off him strong. I gave him a slow, pleasant smile when I noticed that he was wearing matching pajamas—very rare for a man in these mountains—that had little boats printed in different colors, and of different types of vessels, all over the pajamas. I knew better than to say anything about them, and didn't.

I said hello, and asked him his name. To which he replied with a bird-like cawing and high-pitched throat mumbling, followed by coughing and more head wobbling. Then he opened the outside aluminum storm door to the trailer.

He opened the door with a rusted to doubtful brown double-barreled shotgun, an ancient 12-gauge J.C. Higgins model.

And there we were. Me and him. My Vodka Boatman and I, together at last for our momentous, yet strangely calm meeting under a brilliant October sky. Beyond all time that had stopped, beyond all space that had melted away from us, we were alone, vivid and terrifying to each other, two strangers suddenly trapped by fate. Like a pair of misshapen pixies inside a snow globe, we were imprisoned by the crystalline fragility to that kind of threshold experience that seems to forebode REALLY BAD SHIT is about to happen.

The Vodka Boatman—he was squawking and swallowing his chin down in gulps, and the gun barrels kept angling up and turning towards me.

I slammed the screen door against the shotgun, pinning the long barrels against the doorway jamb. But aimed by some diabolical strength, the deadly twin pipes rose up inexorably and pivoted again, pointing towards my gut.

I leaned on the cheap-ass screen door so hard that the door was actually *bending* around the shotgun.

Don't ask me why I was using the door, and not trying to grab the barrels with my hands instead. For that matter, don't ask me why I kept hearing someone hollering, someone who sounded like me but further off in the distance and very tinny sounding, someone who kept yelling desperately, louder and louder above the sound of blood beating inside my ears, someone screaming repeatedly at the demented old drooler: "THINK ABOUT IT, MISTER! JUST THINK ABOUT IT!"

Chapter Twenty-Three

Saved by Doomed Pigs:
My Last Assignment

It was 12 January 2004, and it was my last assignment.

I was mildly lost somewhere in the maze of rural roads that sprawl between the NC border and Clayton, Georgia. My surveillance subject was nowhere in sight. More than fifteen minutes had passed since my last visual contact. Driving with my truck windows down, my head poked outside the cab, I was frantically sniffing the clean winter air for the smell of pigshit.

Usually an unwelcome odor, pigshit. But in this instance, it would lead me to the triumphant resolution of both the surveillance effort and my career as a P.I.

But at that particular moment, I had that sinking feeling that I had blown it. Worse, I predicted that very scenario.

Back in November 2002, I performed a preliminary due diligence assessment of medical malpractice disability claimant John Daniel "JD" Shuford. Shuford had visited a chiropractor in March 2001, and suffered a stroke as the result of the spinal manipulation he received there. He was allegedly temporarily totally disabled, with one side of his body feeble and uncoordinated. According to his attorney, he required the use of a mobility cart. I tried to determine through drive-by activity checks and a search of his background whether the subject's true physical activity level might be demonstrated at his residence, which was tucked inside the hollers of Patton Mountain down in Macon County.

At that time, all I could come up with was a mixed bag. I could find no evidence that he was gainfully employed outside the home after March 2001. Yet in September 2002 he had purchased a '01 GMC truck and paid cash for it. He lived in a home owned by his father, and lived there alone after his divorce. He held a current, unlimited hunting license and yet he had not filed for a handicapped endorsement. Neighbors advised that he was an avid 'coon hunter, but his truck bore no hunting dog boxes, and there were no 'coon dogs on his place. His truck also did not have a handicapped parking placard or license plate, and his house had no ramps attached to the elevated front and back porch decks—ramps that would indicate the use of a mobility cart.

One thing was clear, however: there would be no protracted surveillance of Shuford's activities around his home. In my preliminary report, my boilerplate pessimism read like this:

At this time, this investigator believes that any protracted surveillance effort directed towards capturing this subject's physical activity level—as it might be demonstrated in or around the subject's residence—would encounter an extremely high risk of detection and/or evasion by the subject himself.

Translation: You ain't gonna get nothing by watching this guy except caught.

The greater Shuford clan—brothers, sisters, father, cousins—all lived on adjacent parcels that virtually surrounded the subject's small house which was located on an elevated hill that overlooked a narrow dead end road. The Shufords owned from ridgetop to ridgetop across the valley in the shadow of Patton Mountain. Over time, the family acreage had been subdivided as their membership increased. Once you headed down Mashburn White Road and crossed the Cartoogechaye Creek, you were in Shuford Country. Every vantage point, every wooded tangle, every pile of moldy haybales, every roadside—was either their property or directly in their purview. And even if one could dismiss the consequences of trespassing or otherwise ignoring the message behind the pointed stares of kinfolks peering out of trailer windows or standing on porches—the features of the land, itself, could not be overlooked. The land was cleared for farming along the rolling bottom near the roadway, then rose steep and fast and plunged into woods so dense that you would have to climb quite a ways up a tree to be able to see the houses below and still avoid being seen yourself.

And being treed while illegally on the land of 'coon hunters—while trying to deprive one of their kin of his lifetime disability settlement—didn't seem like much of an option.

Attempting to follow Shuford if and when he left the family compound would not be much of an option, either. The meandering two lane roads that coiled around the mountains were interconnected by private drives and strange unmarked road spurs that served as either ingenious multiple shortcuts towards four-lane highways or as hair-raising dead ends atop cliff edges or overgrown creekbeds. A local boy like Shuford could lose you without even trying or worse, deliberately lead you to a place where you couldn't turn around. Then he could double-back on you and cut you off and there you would be, blocked by his vehicle, trapped. Your surveillance effort was burned, and a humiliating exchange along the following lines would be the best you could do:

"Naw, I wasn't following you, not really. All right, maybe I was following you. But I am not supposed to talk to you, because you're represented by an attorney and all. I hate having to do these things, but I was just seeing if you're okay, and you are, so if you'll please move your truck, I'll be on my way, directly."

Yet for all that, the attorney for the chiropractor—really the attorney for the chiropractor's insurance carrier—felt that the plaintiff's account of his own current physical limitations seemed incomplete. So just before Christmas 2003, the attorney had called me.

"Brian, what do you think about doing some surveillance on Shuford after the holidays?"

"Not much."

I reiterated the concerns I raised the year before, and he acknowledged their validity. But his client wanted something definite one way or the other before they settled with Shuford. I told him that a few discreet drive-by activity checks might pick up something, and that I was willing—weather permitting—to try my luck at some passive mobile surveillance, i.e., parking in an overgrown ditch somewhere overlooking one of *three* possible routes Shuford might take to go do something off-farm, and just hope for the best.

My lack of enthusiasm for the assignment was of parts. Part of me thought it would be a waste of time and a further harassment of some unlucky country boy with a permanently wry neck; part of me could certainly use the money but didn't want to get shot or hassled excessively to earn it.

And another part of me was pondering whether to leave the business altogether.

My morale was virtually nonexistent. I was beginning to dread the ring of the business phone. The past fall's encounter with the Vodka Boatman and the cumulative effect of my protracted MomWatch had combined with an increasing workload to make me feel raw and jittery as soon as I awoke. And that was just for starters.

My monthly numbers proved that I was working longer hours yet somehow earning less on each case. Law firms were demanding more for their client's money and balking at advancing retainer payments. Lawyers were also relying more and more upon their own paralegals and commercial databases to perform witness locates and interviews. These in-house moves eliminated a sizable source of my reliable, relatively uncomplicated assignments.

Other corporate clients had started playing harder hardball, too. They were searching for the lowest cost "contractor" regardless of results; they were delaying payments up to ninety days on some complex cases in which I had incurred considerable credit card expenses, the interest on which gnawed away at my cash flow and my peace of mind. To pay the bills, I took on more surveillance assignments and asset recovery work, the latter of which were grueling, nerve-wracking affairs (remember Sonny the Helldog? That's what I'm talking about). Non-domestic private pay clients who were both sane *and* financially solvent were diminishing. For private pays, Google had replaced gumshoes. Domestic cases were still a plentiful mess; however, there were more hungry P.I.'s chasing them.

I was sleeping less and worrying more. I had too little ego left to cushion the daily blows. I had spent sixteen years hiding and diminishing my own sense of self in order to blend in with others. I had succeeded. I was disappearing before my eyes.

For several months in a row, it seemed, I could be found staring into the bathroom mirror at four in the morning and declaring softly "I am quitting because. . ." and waiting to see what my face would give for an answer.

Because . . . I am so tired of being tired. Either I have to do everything in seconds . . . or do nothing for hours and hours at a time.

Because. . . my gift of knowing what's wrong with this picture is actually a curse . . . and I want it to end.

Because. . . living a shadow life where "Ye shall know me by my website visits and business receipts" is no way to go through life.

Because . . . I need to quit while I still can.

The Thrill Fiends—adrenaline rush, danger addiction, whatever you want to call the insatiable creatures summoned by the realization that sweats through your skin—*Wow! I could get killed doing this!*—hadn't fully consumed me yet. Just in time, I think, I recognized the signs that said stop. There was Linda to consider in all of this, of course, but there was someone else I wanted to save from the all-consuming investigator's world.

One day long ago it seemed that I had jumped on this career train. As it picked up speed, I never had the time to figure out where it was going or how indeed I could jump off safely. I was scared to jump and even more scared not to.

Come New Year's Eve, I had decided to jump. *Why drag it out?* The first of February or March would give me enough time to notify my long-term clients, shut down my website, disconnect the extra phone lines.

And I knew I would surrender my license, too.

I sensed that once I blurred my focus, once I blunted my edge, I was finished. I didn't want to be one of those P.I.'s who stayed in the game long past their effectiveness. The profession is no place for dilettantes, even though they are every-where. The profession is littered with folks who just want to "keep their hand in it," as they say. They cherry-pick domestic assignments, dabbling here and there in occasional locates, posturing as an expert who is too busy for low-dollar cases while secretly hoping no one ever challenges the modest limits of their authority and expertise with really tricky assignments. I felt sorry for most of them, but I definitely did not want to emulate them.

As long as I held that license, I would always find an excuse to return to this gig. Some friends in a jam. The money got tight. My mind just needed some-thing to chew on. I did not need to be licensed to work for a single attorney or law firm, true enough. But to me, the symbolic act of surrendering my license would be the strongest statement that I was removing myself from the constant temptation posed by the "Truth Fairy," who would show up on my pillow at night, whispering lurid tales of mysteries that only Brian Lee Knopp could solve. . . .

I had several minor cases to wrap up before I could quit: witness locates and background checks that didn't risk any face-to-face confrontations. There was the usual blizzard of process service assignments that fell around Christmas time: "*Merry Christmas, glad to see that you came home to visit your folks—so here's a big, brand new lawsuit against you, ho ho ho, gotta go!*" These I referred to other inves-tigators.

And I still had the Shuford mess to contend with—and I didn't want to con-tend with it at all. Like combat soldiers who get more superstitious and nervous the closer they get to leaving the battlefield, I didn't really want another high-risk surveillance operation while I was distracted by the prospects of—well, unem-ployment, actually—but mostly I saw it as freedom.

The Shuford assignment, Part II, had started out as so many winter surveil-lance details do: loading up and checking my equipment before dawn in the dark cracking cold; driving for hours through the sleeping mountains; stopping at an all-night truck stop so I could gas up, clean my windows and mirrors and re-check my equipment before I arrived within a half-hour's driving time from the subject's residence. I had waited through a week of icy rain and then impulsively com-mitted to the first day when it would clear, hoping that if Shuford had any farm chores or firewood to work, I might catch him doing it.

But as dawn pushed the night off the land, I could see that all was frozen. The vehicles glazed with ice. The pastures and forests sparkled like enameled metal. Rhododendron leaves drooped down and curled tightly into tubes. My heart first lifted from the beauty of it all and then sank with the realization *too cold*. Way colder than the "chance of scattered light frost" the weather forecast had prom-ised. Very few able-bodied folks would choose to work outside on a morning like this, maybe turning out around noon. If Shuford's body was actually as stoved up as he claimed, he might never go out at all.

My turnoff from US 64 onto Mashburn White Road loomed up ahead, so I turned off all my internal chatter and prepared for an initial drive-by activity check of Shuford's residence, which was less than three miles away. It was 07:30 hours, still a little too dark to pick up much with my pursuit camera. I had turned the pursuit camera sideways, aimed at the passenger's window in order to capture whatever was visible or happening within a field of view from the immediate roadside on my right on out to 100 yards. But I turned it on anyway, making sure it worked and that the focus was correct. I used its time display to synchronize my truck's dashboard clock, the watch on my wrist, the stopwatch strapped to the steering wheel, and the internal clock on my hand-held videocamera. As I headed on up the shadowy holler towards Shuford's place, I recorded the date, time, ambient weather conditions for this first activity check. I wanted to drive by slow and look around in the weak morning light, so I could figure out what the subject may have planned for the day without attracting attention.

The house was on my left and it was . . . dark, still sleeping in the shadows of Patton Mountain. No lights on, no activity observed. Parked off to the right of the driveway was the subject's blue 1991 Chevy truck. There was a 1992 blue Ford Mustang parked in the driveway. From my earlier due diligence effort I knew that the Mustang belonged to his brother, Luke Shuford. A green 4-wheeler sat on the frosted lawn. Across the road from the house was a single-story barn cluttered with tractor implements and livestock equipment and Shuford's 2001 GMC truck. It was backed into the paddock next to the barn, and through the front windshield I saw the silver outline of a radio signal tracking antenna, the kind hunters use to locate the radio transmitters affixed to hunting dog collars. I also observed that the truck was outfitted with a metal hunting dog housing box located in the truck bed. Located on top of the dog box was a tie rail and several tie leads used to secure hunting dogs.

Well, that's interesting . . . it was almost mid-January and the winter 'coon hunting season still had another month to go, and it looked like ole JD had been hunting. He may have just been driving around tracking the dogs and not actually "going to the dogs." That is, he might not be actually clambering around the mountains to find what the dogs had treed. He might have been the one driving and had someone sitting next to him sticking the antenna out the passenger's window. So all in all, the tracking antenna didn't speak to his current physical activity level or abilities. But it did speak to the enjoyment of life value of his claim, and if he could still indulge in his passion for coon hunting, the defense attorney would be able to take a couple thousand dollars from him down the road.

But there was something else about the truck that caught my eye on this frosty morning: the front windshield was clear. The windows had been scraped and defrosted, and not too long ago. And most notable of all—there was a livestock trailer hooked to the back of the truck.

I pondered Shuford's truck as I continued on up the holler, turning my lights off as I turned around in front of the dead-end house—a house owned by a Shuford relative—and then coasted silently back down the hill. My truck and I rolled through the darkness until I found a place off the road where, with the help of binoculars, I could watch the barn and GMC truck.

The spot I chose—a small flattened hump just a few feet off the road's shoulder that had a few scraggly rhododendron bushes hanging over at the height of truck's cab—was so obvious that I realized I could not stay there all day. I really didn't want to park there at all, as I was trapped between JD's place and the dead-end, with no real exits available. But I had to be able see what might happen with that truck. From that site, I could not see the trailer, as it was obscured by objects in the foreground. But that didn't matter. The trailer wouldn't be going anywhere without the truck, and whoever worked with the trailer would have to walk to the truck. The lower yard and driveway area of the Shuford residence was likewise hidden from my view. But I could see the house itself. Anyone walking in or out of the front door would catch my eye.

Around 08:00 hrs, two vehicles drove past me and proceeded down the hill, each bearing a single female driver and a small child as a passenger. The women could have been twins. Their mouths were set in the same thin gashes across their identical puffy faces, their hair piled atop their heads like arguments. Neither driver paid any attention to my vehicle.

And after that, nothing happened for over two hours. Except that the sun finally climbed over the mountains and shot bright diamonds through my front windshield, through my binoculars and straight through to the back of my skull, or so it seemed.

At 10:00 hrs, I was effectively a blind sitting duck there on the side of the road. The only workable vantage point from which I had hoped to monitor activity around the truck was gone. Gone, that is, until close to noon, when the sun would be out of my eyes and I could return to this rather blatant surveillance site.

With a sigh I resigned myself to conducting several drive-by activity checks over the next two hours.

These activity checks ran the risk of tipping off my subject, of course. But I might luck out and see him doing strenuous activity, and then hopefully I could get a minute or two of it on film as I passed by. Maybe I'd spot him leaving in his truck, and by following him I might catch him loading bags of dog food or livestock feed. Or maybe he would be so incapacitated by his injuries that one of his kin was using his truck and trailer and I'd wind up with nothing for my troubles today.

At the least, though, these activity checks would give me a better feel for what

Shuford might have planned for the day.

Weather-wise, the day was turning out to be splendid. Surveillance-wise, it was looking pretty bleak. Tooling up and down a dead-end road repeatedly in front of JD and all his kin would probably not even deliver an entire day's work. In all likelihood, I would get eyeballed and suspected. To avoid a confrontation, I would have to make the judgment call to terminate surveillance and subsequently drive home with very little to show for my last investigative assignment.

I tumbled out of my truck and moved stiffly from the cold and inactivity. I carried two magnetized plastic signs clutched in my hands. I slapped one on each truck door and crawled back in the truck and started the engine. The day seemed like a good day to be a cable TV installer, which was what the phony signs suggested I might be up to while driving back and forth all day on the same stretch of road. I ruled out the pretext of surveyor, because that would surely alarm the Shuford clan, given the nature of the subdivided land parcels surrounding me. They might even try to flag me down and find out whose land I was surveying. The signs were merely part of my attempt to deflect any undue attention; if they actually invited inquiries, my attempt at deception would have been worse than futile.

I drove down the hill for what would be my first drive-by activity check. The time was 10:15 hrs. Because the truck and trailer were to my left, I could not use the pursuit camera. Instead, I was holding my handheld videocamera with my right hand, with the camera body tucked under my left arm which was holding the steering wheel. I aimed the camera toward the partially-opened window and braced it against my chest and underneath my left arm. I knew the range and depth-of-field which I'd be filming and so I adjusted the focus well before I got very far down the hill.

As I was filming to my left, I was actually looking in the opposite direction, towards my right side—the side on which the subject's house was located. As I closed to within a hundred yards or so of the subject's house, I noted that a teal Ford pickup was now parked close to the mouth of the driveway—a truck that I did not recognize as belonging to JD. It was parked off the road, facing me, so I wouldn't be able to see the license plate until I passed by. I grabbed my dictaphone in my left hand so I could note the plate as I drove by—but then a whitish blur to the left caught my eye. I turned my head slightly and *Shit! Was that him?* I first saw the white baseball cap drifting slowly along the field. Then I took in the long-sleeved camouflaged hunting jacket and the tan Carhartt-type pants.

The white hat was less than thirty feet away.

As I drove away from him I glanced to the right, towards Shuford's house. Driving by the house, I punched the record button on the dictaphone and blurted out the plate of the teal Ford pickup as I passed by—

—"NC tag Edward X-ray Tom Thirty Forty-eight!"

I recorded the time of the white hat sighting. I set the stopwatch function on the wristwatch attached to my steering wheel, so I would know how long to either wait for Shuford's truck to appear driving down the road or to drive back towards the barn to figure out who White Hat was and what White Hat may be up to.

And as I drove at a crawl down the road, beyond sight range of the subject's residence, I was reviewing the video footage I just took . . . and I swear it looked as if White Hat limped. For several frames White Hat was seen taking an exaggerated, awkward step over some object in the field, and dropping his shoulder down in time with an excessive bend to his knee on the same side. He walked like someone who had just felt the weight of a heavy bag dropped on his shoulder and he buckled slightly from the sudden strain.

But White Hat wasn't carrying anything.

Glancing occasionally in my rearview mirror, and in front of me, too, from time to time, to keep from driving off the road into a tree, I reviewed the footage again while describing the scene to my dictaphone.

But then as the video flickered on, I saw something else that almost made me swerve off the road.

The trailer attached to the pickup was no longer empty. Two enormous white hogs were stuffed literally cheek by jowl between the trailer's side rails. Under the brilliant sun they looked like big piles of dirty snow.

No! No way!

Someone had pushed two pigs the size of sofas into the trailer—and I had missed it. I had lost out on capturing the big activity of the day.

Before my mind could descend into an irrevocable downward spiral of frustration and self-recrimination, I puzzled over how and when and by whom the pigs might have been loaded.

I swerved into the first empty driveway I saw and parked. I checked my stopwatch. Seven minutes had elapsed from the time I first saw White Hat. Keeping my eyes glued to my rearview mirror, in case truck, trailer and porkers passed by, I punched the number for NC Department of Motor Vehicles into my cell phone and prayed for both a clear signal and a direct ring through to an operator.

I called in the plate for the teal Ford pickup. The truck turned out to be registered to Roger Lee Shuford, at an address just up the hill past JD's residence. I closed up the cell phone and ground my fists into my bloodshot eyes to help push my thoughts along. But too much thinking on a cold, empty stomach was giving me a headache. I looked again at the stopwatch – twenty minutes had passed. I decided to give the White Pig Express until noon to drive by. At noon, I'd go back up to my previous surveillance site and see what would happen from there.

I suddenly hurt all over, as if I was thawing out too quickly from earlier in the day when it was below freezing. Or maybe it was the crushing realization that I had somehow missed the Shuford Show, so to speak, and that meant my last surveillance assignment would be a dud.

I tallied up the score. According to my subject's most recent IME (independent medical exam), his current impairment rating did not prohibit him from driving. So filming him driving his truck would prove little. With the presence of another vehicle and possibly as many as two other phantom assistants, the miracle of loaded pigs could be accounted for without impugning his disability. The brief video footage seemed to suggest an awkward, even spastic-kind of movement affecting the same side of the body that Shuford complained of after his stroke. But White Hat might have just stumbled at the same time he looked away from the ground to waive at the passing cable TV contractor.

And I had no idea who White Hat really was.

Score: Shuford 5, Knopp 0.

HARRP!

The honk of a car's horn made me damn near swallow my tongue. I flicked my eyes in startled disbelief towards the rearview mirror.

There was an elderly couple in a blue Buick behind me. The woman driver was pursing her lips expectantly. The man in the passenger seat was shaking his head with a Parkinson's rhythm, staring out his side window, looking far off in the distance. The Buick was angled across the road and towards the driveway I was blocking. *Their* driveway.

I started my truck, gave a brief nod and wave, then drove away from the last relatively safe surveillance site.

And then a panicked thought raced through me, electrifying me more than the car horn.

What if Shuford brought the hogs home? He could be unloading them now!

I glanced at the stopwatch—twenty-five minutes.

Of course, that possibility made no sense. Who picks up pigs in the dark, drives them back to their farm, and lets them sit there jammed together in a trailer for hours?

It was too warm and too late in the day for slaughtering now.

No, they were taking the pigs somewhere.

I had to make some decisions. It was almost 10:45. The sun was still too bright for me to get decent shots of any activity around the truck and barn. Of course, I now know that not much activity could occur there, anyway, without me seeing it, sunshine or not. If I went back to my previous site, I would at least see the truck leaving.

From my previous due diligence efforts, I knew that I couldn't cover all the ways Shuford might soon travel with the pigs. I'd have to decide in advance upon the most likely route and wait him out. A roll of the dice was just the way it would have to be.

So I drove back up the road towards the subject's house. I clicked on my pursuit camera to record the barn area as I drove by. The teal Ford pickup was gone from JD's house, but I saw it parked later on at what would seem to be Roger's house.

As I passed by the rear of Roger's house—there was White Hat, talking to a stockily-built fellow dressed in blue jeans, and a dark blue jacket. The man in blue had a full dark beard and thick black hair bushing out underneath a light-tan baseball cap. I glimpsed the two of them briefly before the woods around the house swallowed them up. I could not tell if they saw me drive by or not.

I drove to the dead-end, turned around and returned to my surveillance site. After recording my observations, I reset the stopwatch. And I did nothing for the next four hours but sit. Nibbled on a Cliffs Bar. Drank water. Peed it back out. Watched the little winter birds—finches, nuthatches, titmice—flit among the trees.

I did not risk more drive-by activity checks for fear of spooking Shuford, if that indeed was the man wearing the White Hat. I would wait for that GMC truck—until dark, if necessary—to move those pigs, and I would hope for the remote chance of seeing White Hat do some sort of physical activity.

At approximately 14:30 hrs, I saw the school bus lumbering towards the Shuford residence. Except for the two women driving their kids in the morning and the old couple in the Buick, there had not been any vehicle traffic all day until now, a fact for which—given my exposed position—I was extremely grateful. The school bus crawled up the hill and stopped below where Roger's house was located. Then the bus disappeared. But I could still hear the diesel engine throbbing as it pulled up the hill. I heard the brakes squeal, indicating another stop, and then I saw it coming toward me. The man driving the bus looked me over as he passed by, and I waved at him. There were no kids left on the bus, and he'd be turning around and leaving here, anyway. I figured that I had arrived here after his morning run, so I didn't worry about him seeing me there. A man who was a stranger to the area could not stop and hang out by himself near bus stops without attracting scrutiny. A sign of the times, even in rural North Carolina.

But after the bus turned around at the dead-end and motored on down the hill below me, it stopped a ways past Roger's house. It stopped for several minutes—ten minutes, actually. And it stopped directly in between my line of sight toward Shuford's GMC truck.

So then I did start to worry a little bit about the bus driver seeing me.

Call it coincidence. Call it conspiracy. Call it just plain bad luck. But when the bus finally lurched away in a puff of blue smoke, the GMC truck was nowhere in sight.

I jumped out of my truck and pulled the magnetic signs off—didn't need them anymore. I would just lose them in what looked like an imminent chase for a vanished GMC truck and a 16-foot livestock trailer full of pork.

I fired up my truck and took off down the hill.

As I passed by the barn, I couldn't believe my eyes.

It was gone. The big gray truck with the tracking antennae and dog boxes and 16-foot trailer and the hogs—all gone. There were muddy tracks leading out of the holler, and I followed them all the way toward Mashburn White, but they petered out before I could get to the intersection.

Which way did he go? Think, Brian!

Would he turn onto Patton Road on his way toward US Highway 64 and then probably toward Franklin and a meat processing plant there?

There were three ways he could turn and I couldn't cover them all. But the route to Franklin seemed the most likely.

I tried the Franklin theory. I turned up Mashburn White and shifted into neutral and coasted silently down a hill at about 30 mph. I rolled down the windows to listen, hoping to hear . . . something . . . other than my own thoughts quarreling.

Hey, good show! You lost, what, only the biggest moving object you've ever had to follow in sixteen years?

C'mon, this is your last assignment. You're getting paid no matter what. You made no promises to the attorney. So you lost him—big hairy deal.

It IS a big hairy deal.

I spat in frustration out the window, feeling the brisk air scouring the inside of the truck. Beautiful mountain air.

Wait. Something's up.

I swerved onto the shoulder and stopped. The wind flooded inside the truck again and filled up my nostrils.

That's it! I smell it!

Pigshit.

I threw the truck in gear and floored it, wheels spinning in the thawed mud of the road shoulder, tires flinging mud clumps everywhere and then the chirp of traction as the rubber hit the road.

The scent was stronger now and the wind was blowing from the southeast.

So that means . . . ahhhh, he didn't go up Mashburn White, he went, uh . . . .

I fumbled for the hotsheet page with the Macon County streetmap excerpt photocopied onto it—and realized that White Hat was going in the other direction. He took Patton Ridge Road!

I threw the gearshift into neutral and pulled the emergency brake and did a bootlegger's turn in the middle of Mashburn White. The abrupt U-turn hurled my gear around and I reached back with one hand, patting signal cords and electrical connections back in place to make sure everything was still hooked up. I drove in the oncoming lane of the curve to cut the corners faster to make up for time.

40 . . . 50 . . . 60 mph . . . and then screeched to a halt at an intersection.

141

Did he go down Dobson Road to the right?

Sniff sniff sniff – I didn't smell anything.

Why would he go down Dobson Road—for a private sale of the hogs? No, too close to his house—someone would just come get them. Go on!

I drove on.

30-40-50 – 60 – 70 and stopped again at the intersection of Jones Ridge Road.

Sniff sniff sniff sniff

Pigshit.

As I flew down Jones Ridge Road, I glanced quickly at the hotsheet again. Jones Ridge led right to US 23–441, a four-lane that ran north directly to Franklin and south to the Georgia border that was only a few miles away.

Jones Ridge twisted and turned then intersected with US 23-441. I dug out my binoculars and scanned the northbound lane for a few seconds, watching cars disappear and reappear as they bobbed up and down in the distance along the hilly roadway. I saw nothing at first.

Then there was the boxlike silhouette of a livestock trailer, with the just faint outline of gray in front of it, moving down the southbound lane almost a half a mile away.

Cackling with glee, speeding down the highway 50 –60 –70 -80, I swung the pursuit camera toward the front windshield, checked the focus, readied my hand-held camera.

All of a sudden, I noticed the auxiliary battery had died. My cameras were off.

Nosir. You're not getting away that easy. Not after all the shit I've been through today.

I wiggled around in my seat as I zoomed down the highway, frantically unplugging my cameras from the auxiliary battery and patching them directly into the truck's own electricity via the cigarette lighter.

Then I noticed something else. The LED status display for the pursuit camera was flashing the symbol for internal condensation! The camera would not function because of the drastic temperature change that day from below freezing to over 70 degrees inside the truck.

Everything would have to be shot with the handheld. It is no mean feat to take smooth video of a vehicle in front of you when you are bouncing and swerving around behind it. But I had no choice.

I gained on the truck and trailer. Driving with one hand, the camera pushed into my chest for stability and sighting down the LED display, I took establishing shots of the vehicle going south on the highway, and entered the time in the dictaphone. I slowed down to the legal limit and kept the truck and trailer a quarter mile ahead of me with several cars between us.

I followed the truck and trailer for over a half hour as it crossed the NC/GA state line, then turned left onto Larry McClure Valley Road, proceeded down the winding Kelly's Creek Road, and pulled into Blalock's Meat Processing facility. At Blalock's I found out that White Hat was the passenger. A taller fellow who bore a strong resemblance to White Hat was driving.

So which one is my subject claimant? Would JD allow someone else to drive his truck?

I decided to film them both. I filmed them while they were unloading the hogs, climbing over fencing stiles, pushing heavy gates, walking back and forth around the facility, waiting for someone to let them back their trailer in the corral. When they left the meat processing facility around 15:30 hrs, I followed them to a gas station where they bought sodas and filled the truck with gas. Both subjects moved easily, without showing any signs of favoring a limb, altered gait, or one-sided weakness. I followed them all the way back to Patton Mountain, where I eventually determined that White Hat was JD Shuford. Because I heard him called by his name.

* * * * * *

The day's triumph would be celebrated in my head without much fanfare. There was no one around to share my exhilaration of the moment. By the time I arrived home, that exhilaration had faded into the fitful exhaustion of a fourteen-hour day. And what exactly would I have celebrated, anyway? Like thousands of P.I.'s across the country, I had simply persevered until a bad day turned into good. That's all there was to it.

No. There was more to it than that. I got my mojo back. I would be quitting on top, with a successful surveillance detail. I had been redeemed by doomed pigs.

On the long drive back home, I wrestled again with my decision to quit.

I would miss the rush that came with certain assignments, the all-consuming high of plunging into the chaos with the throb and hum of hyper-awareness and single-minded purpose. Being a P.I. was as addictive as any extreme sport, a sort of mental whitewater kayaking in which you risked being pummeled and sucked down to the depths of the storm surge that is human behavior.

I would not miss the lows at all. And although my math skills were poor, the calculus of my P.I. experience seemed obvious to me: the lows outnumbered the highs by a wide margin.

I wanted to free myself from my obsession for searching in the dark for all the broken pieces to human jigsaw puzzles that wouldn't stay together, anyhow. I no longer wanted to hear, see and remember *everything*. I wanted to *forget* once in awhile, and forget without dreadful consequences.

I wanted to forget The Vodka Boatman.

When I came home, Linda had just arrived from work minutes before. She greeted me at the door.

"Hello. How'd it go?" she asked with a kiss.

"Good. I lost him for a bit but I found him again. The pigshit helped."

She looked at me quizzically and sniffed at me. "Do I want to know more?"

"No, probably not."

"So that's it? You're done? That was your last case, right?"

"Yep."

"Yay! How do you feel about it all?"

I didn't know. There was so much ahead, yet so much I wanted to put behind, I felt cut in two, rather than free and whole. I didn't know that the worst was yet to come for my mother. And for me. Quitting my profession just allowed me more time to focus on her, if "focus" is the right description for the passive, anxiety-ridden, oh-no-here-we-go-again kind of protracted watchfulness that I performed. Brian Lee Knopp, the former surveillance expert, would now watch and wait for psychotic episodes.

"How do you feel about it all?"

How would I feel when the phone rang late Sunday night? The time husbands with cheating wives called. The time subcontract P.I.'s called to bail out on my Monday morning surveillance detail. The time a demented aging mother would call, when the empty nest of her life invited fear to fill the void.

How would I feel when the phone stopped ringing? What would *I* invite in to fill the void in my professional life?

In the end, I was shocked to discover that my workaday P.I. philosophy and the moral imperative behind all of my efforts to care for my mother turned out to be the same: *you simply persevered until a bad day turned into good. That was all there was to it. That's all anyone can do.*

"How do you feel about it all?"

I think I know now.

Acknowledgements

First and foremost, I would like to thank my mother, Inez Eileen Knopp, June 19, 1930-May 15, 2006. Without her, none of me would be possible.

I am profoundly indebted to the native mountain folk of western North Carolina for sharing their habits and heritage with me.

I had excellent readers: Elizabeth Gilbert, Jeff Biggers, David Schenck, Ph.D., Maria Fire and Calvin Allen, Monica Nolan and Tom Kilby, Gretchen Horn, and Georgia Smith. My gratitude for their time, patience, wisdom, and good-humored handling of me and my memoir is without measure.

Monster thanks, also, to Emöke B'Racz and the rest of the crew at Malaprop's Bookstore/Café. You who have always inspired me not to forget the creative side, no matter how painful it might be, are not forgotten.

Kasey Gruen was not deterred by the demands of her newborn son and did a super job on the graphic design.

Odin the Pit Bull. Good dog!

Finally, there is The One, the Monad, The WünderStoat, my beautiful, talented, all-seeing, all-knowing wife and excellent editor Linda Barrett Knopp, who saves the day, every day. What more can I say?

About the Author

Brian Lee Knopp has provided legal support investigations, both criminal and civil, for over twenty years in North Carolina. His clients have ranged from huge corporate law firms to the indigent. He is a former professional sheep shearer with an M.A. degree in English Literature from The University of Texas at Austin. For the past twenty-one years he has lived in the mountains north of Asheville, North Carolina. His book reviews and essays have been published in several regional magazines and local media. As a licensed P.I., sheep shearer, and avid outdoorsman, he has roamed extensively throughout western North Carolina.

Interview with the Author

Why did you write this book?

This memoir was my attempt to explain to others what it was like to be a P.I. in western North Carolina from 1996-2004—and in the process, to finally understand for myself why I chose to give it up in 2004, in spite of my peculiar aptitude for the job.

What is this book about?

The book focuses primarily upon my experiences as a P.I. in western North Carolina and upon certain events that occurred in my life during 2003-2004 that led up to my decision to surrender my P.I. license. But I also draw from both life events and investigations that occurred before that time period.

The heart of the book is about accepting the stark truth that life can sucker-punch you and make you doubt all of your skills, courage, and hard work, and that you have to persevere to find a creative way to overcome it. Writing this memoir was my way to make sense of—and to make peace with—my P.I. experience.

What did you like best about being a P.I.?

The rush I always got from having to figure out strange people, animals, and machines within seconds--or else I would be in big trouble! Also, if you have an odd or dark sense of humor, being a P.I. can be hilarious. It's a gig like no other; it can bring you so close—and sometimes over—the edge, time after time. And you get paid for it. It's like getting paid for bungee jumping or tickling tigers. Simply awesome.

What did you like least about being a P.I?

The business end of it. It is a highly competitive, utterly unforgiving, very cutthroat, back-stabbing business. Excellent service is no guarantee of success or longevity in the business. The profession is not for worriers. But then, if you're not a worrier, you probably won't make it as a P.I. for very long or be very effective—and you might just get killed. It's a paradox, but there it is, the P.I. profession thrives on paradox.

What was your greatest achievement as a P.I.?

If I had to name my one greatest achievement as a P.I., I guess it would be a toss-up between one case in which I actually tracked down someone by smell alone—that case informs the last chapter of my memoir—and another case in which I found a gun hidden in the woods that several teams of deputies and their search dogs couldn't find. I felt very dog-like and quite proud of myself on those occasions.

In general, I am delighted to have survived all the bizarre and potentially lethal encounters over the years. P.I.'s often have very dubious achievements. Sometimes your greatest sleuthing and feats of derring-do ultimately accomplish nothing and save no one. And then there's no one you can tell your success stories to, because of client confidentiality and professional discretion. So you have to keep redefining your victories and celebrate them in silence.

What was your worst moment as a P.I.?

Well, I write about that moment in my memoir—when I had to use all of my P.I. skills to try and help my mother, who was suffering from dementia. But I couldn't save her.

What type of assignments did you like best as a P.I.?

I loved being outdoors, and so anytime I was getting paid to do things like horseback riding, kayaking, or skulking about in the dark quiet woods for days at a time—it was all good. I loved high risk rural surveillance, where you had to go deep into the forests to document fraudulent or illegal activities. It combined all the best features of hunting, hiking, and pure adrenaline rushes. In general, though, I loved interviewing witnesses. The verbal and nonverbal chess game that is human communication never grows old or stale. I was extremely blessed to find myself in a region of the country where I could be challenged by so many cunning and entertaining talkers.

What type of assignments did you like least?

Domestic assignments. Infidelity, child custody, child abuse—always a painful mess.

I am tempted to add serving civil process. Serving legal papers was the most consistently dangerous and unpredictable thing I did in the mountains. The only times I ever had people pull guns on me or actively try to harm me in some way was during process service attempts. You just never know what you've walked into stepping on that porch with that piece of paper in your hand, or what you'll likely touch off by handing over that piece of paper. Getting killed for a measly $50 and reimbursable mileage just sucks to contemplate, let alone deal with on a weekly basis.

Who are your writing influences?

Well, I think the period in which writers actually influence how you write occurs very early on in your life, so I can't really say which writer influenced me the most. I mean, the biggest influence on me when I was a child was Warner Bros. cartoons. Not sure how cartoons shaped my prose, but I definitely know how they shaped my outlook on life. But now I don't read writers to be influenced by their style, but just to enjoy them and envy every delightful sentence they craft.

What do you hope to accomplish with this memoir?

Writing and publishing this memoir—in spite of all the adversity and the terrific odds against the whole enterprise—was quite an accomplishment for me. This was a very difficult and problematic book to write. I mean, who would want their first book to focus on some of the most misunderstood and maligned subjects around, and then have them central to one's memoir? P.I.'s and P.I. culture? Southern Appalachia? Mental illness? Minefields, everywhere you look. But I don't think you get to choose the story you have to tell the world—it chooses you. You only get to choose how you tell it, and to whom.

Why did you write a nonfiction memoir, instead of a fiction detective story?

Because my livelihood for the past twenty years has depended upon my ability to construct credible and convincing fact-based narratives about legal matters. That is what I know how to do. The world is so exquisitely weird when you look at it carefully and report it accurately, why would I ever have to make anything up?

What words of advice would you give to someone planning on becoming a P.I.?

For God's sake, get a grip on yourself. Don't do it!

No, in all seriousness, you need to read my book. That's not just ego or self-promotion talking. I've talked with law enforcement officers and other P.I.'s and they've told me there's no book out there like mine. Because I don't pull any punches. My book is not a "how to" but "how it is."

You need to think very carefully about being a P.I. Research thoroughly what P.I.'s actually do, day in and day out. And then try to talk to full-time P.I.'s, their spouses, their family, their friends (if they have any—joke), and ask them about the demands of the profession. Don't settle for the glamour and hype and war stories. If you still want to do it, then God help you. Because after you've been a P.I. for awhile, you can never work a regular nine-to-five gig again. It's like you've become permanently partially disabled or something.

Final warning: being a P.I. leaves you with certain skills, traits, and inclinations that make you virtually unemployable in any non-investigatory capacity. And once you've been a P.I. all the other jobs out there seem boring as hell.

1-8

CPSIA information can be obt
Printed in the USA
LVOW111207130512

281506LV00002E